LARIBA BANK

ISLAMIC BANKING:

FOUNDATION FOR A UNITED AND PROSPEROUS

COMMUNITY

BY: DR. YAHIA KHAIRY
ABDUL RAHMAN

Pasadena, California

Tahrike Tarsile Qur'an, Inc.
80-08 51st Avenue
Elmhurst, New York 11373
Tel: 718.446.6472 Fax: 718.446.4370
www.koranusa.org E-mail: read@koranusa.org

Library of Congress Number
94-70795

ISBN No. 0-911119-97-3

Printed By:
Cedar Graphics, Inc.
P.O. Box 185
Hiawatha, IA 52233
USA

Contents

ACKNOWLEDGMENT

I would like to thank my wife and family for their enduring love, patience and support during the long trying years of developing the concept of LARIBA. Thanks is also due to the many friends who gave their support and trust to participate in the start up, development and growth of American Finance House, LARIBA in California. In addition, the encouragement of Mr. S.A. Kamel and his pioneering creative thoughts on the concept of LARIBA are greatly appreciated.

Mr. Rick St. John contributed his thoughts and editorial remarks during various stages of writing and reviewing this book. The quality of the manuscript is a testament to his hard and quality work. May God bless him and give him success. Thanks also goes to Dr. Hassan Hathout, Mr. Abdullah Tug, Mrs. Ghada Abdel Rahman and Mr. Hassan Igram for their support.

While this book would not have been possible without the help of these and other fine friends, I bear sole responsibility for any errors contained herein.

The people - both Muslims and non - Muslims - whom I have seen working hard to bring peace and justice to this world inspire me to contribute my utmost to these goals.

Ultimately, all thanks and credit for what is good rest in the name of the One, for it is God that gives us the gifts of life, prosperity, and peace.

The author

May, 1994

SECTION I

LARIBA BANKING SYSTEM

BASIC FOUNDATIONS
OF THE SYSTEM

The word LARIBA consists of two parts. These are "LA" which means "NO" and "RIBA" which means the system in which money grows just because it is money, regardless of whether it is used for economic development, speculation or any other objectives. Islam clearly prohibits RIBA. Hence the LARIBA (NO-RIBA) banking system.

This section discusses the basic foundation upon which the LARIBA (Islamic) Banking System is built. These include the business ethics in the Islamic doctrine, discussed in Chapter 2. A brief review of Islamic economics is included in Chapter 3 based on a refreshing treatise by Mr. Sardar in his most interesting book *Islamic Futures*.* Chapter 4 defines the challenge of building a LARIBA bank in a world dominated by RIBA banks.

---

* *Based on a survey which appeared in: Islamic Futures - The Shape of Ideas to Come, Ziauddin Sardar, Chap 9, pp. 198, Pelanduk Publications, Malaysia, 1988.*

CHAPTER ONE

LARIBA BANKING SYSTEM

THE ISLAMIC BANK

The 1980's witnessed the largest bank failures in the history of the United States. The deterioration of the savings and loan industry along with the banking industry itself brought about many pressures for the banks and the savings and loans to compete. Another parallel event was the emergence of money market accounts, by which checking accounts could earn interest on their deposits. With the high interest rates prevailing in the early eighties, many banks and saving and loan associations resorted to speculative lending hoping to achieve higher returns and hence pay the money market accounts, the certificate of deposits and savings accounts those high rates prevailing at that time. When the economy turned from bad to worse and with the recessions of 1987, 1989 and 1990's many of the speculative lending practices were exposed. Many of the troubled banks and savings and loans blamed the economy as the real reason for their failure. It is the author's belief, based on real life experience, consulting for and communicating with many friends and associates in the banking industry, that the real reason for the failure was the lack of moral responsibility on the part of both the lender (lending officers) and the borrower. The real honest businessman was deprived the opportunity of getting his/her loan approved only to find the money going to speculators with special connections to the loan officers or bank management. The result is well known and the damage done not only to the financial markets but also to the whole economy will take years to repair, if not decades.

It is the author's belief that for communities to flourish again and for the economy to restructure in a fundamental and lasting way, moral community banks should be tried once again. History shows that such banks (and building and loan societies) were the real locomotives of community developments in the U.S. out of the Depression during the 1930's. That does not mean that the regional and large money center banks have no place in the economy. Indeed they would be the buyers of the community loan portfolios developed by the community banks.

The step wise approach towards realizing this goal is to create financial institutions which have the capacity of circulating the community savings within the community to activate its economy through financing projects and businesses, and in the process creating job opportunities for the community members and others. The bank would be an honest-to-goodness community development bank which makes money available for non-speculative and economically productive schemes. This is essentially the foundation upon which the concepts of LARIBA (Islamic) banks are built . These concepts are much needed in every part of the world. And because the LARIBA system originated in the Islamic doctrine, it becomes the responsibility of the Muslim

4

communities in America and the West to provide a living example of such a system. If successful, it will present America and the world with an important contribution towards the happiness and prosperity of all people, Muslims and non-Muslims. And the result would be a closer society which is harmonious in its relationships, fair and moral in its dealings, and most productive because it was done right.

This book addresses the LARIBA (Islamic) Banking system. When we describe the Islamic Bank as a LARIBA Bank, we mean the bank which follows the LARIBA Islamic system. Many translate RIBA as interest (The word LARIBA consists of two parts "LA" which means No and "RIBA" which means to grow, connotating the concept of money growing just because it is lent out, regardless of the purpose of lending it. The LARIBA system is a development banking system at heart). We define LARIBA as a system which involves the creation of money (monetary system), the creation of credit (banking and financing) and the total economic system (collection of Zakah,* distribution of inheritance, and most importantly savings).

The contents of this book are based on the author's practical experience accumulated through the start-up, organization and development of American Finance House-LARIBA in Pasadena, California since 1987, in addition to the author's experience in interacting, consulting and doing business with many Islamic banks world-wide.

It is our hope that this preliminary effort will be the beginning of a series of in-depth writings on each of the concepts discussed in this book.

---

 * *A glossary of Islamic words and their meanings is available in the back of this book.*

In conclusion, we ask Almighty God to accept this effort and to forgive us any unintended errors or misconceptions of His system, the LARIBA system of banking and finance.

CHAPTER TWO

ISLAMIC BUSINESS ETHICS

Islam is the religion of submitting our will to the will of God. All Prophets— Abraham, Moses, Jesus and Muhammad (S) (*ppbu-THEM*)— came to train people to be better submittors to God's will and custodians/trustees on God's property; i.e. earth and its resources.

THE ECONOMIC DILEMMA

Human nature, if untamed, is characterized by selfishness and greed. Islam focuses on training the individual spiritually and ethically to suppress selfishness and greed and to promote goodness. The government is responsible for justice, economic justice and justice in all aspects of life. Following, are some important concepts:

Success

Success lies in both material achievements and in being virtuous. Virtue implies a positive attitude towards life and other beings. The results are peace

7

of mind, contentment and a sense of security. The true image of success is not how much money one has in the bank or the kind of car one drives. Success is realizing a track record as a pious person who can be trusted and is close to God; a person who feels for the neediest and the poorest in the community. Success is the progressive realization of a worthy ideal.

Time

The horizon of time in Islam extends beyond this life to the life after death; i.e. the hereafter. Wealth, power, position and affluence do not come with us to our graves after death. When one dies he/she leaves behind (as per Prophet Muhammad's (S) teaching):

- A family and descendants who perpetuate the laws of God.

- A permanent contribution which will benefit the community.

- A source of income for the poor and the needy and/or to generate job opportunities for future generations.

Globe

The globe belongs to God and it is wide open and full of resources and opportunities. Oppression in one location does not justify acceptance. It is the responsibility of everyone, in particular Muslims, to find another location where freedom and human dignity are prevalent. In doing so, a Muslim in his/her pursuit of business, carries with him/her the way of life of Islam.

ELEMENTS OF THE ISLAMIC ECONOMIC SYSTEM

Production

Islam requires every individual to work and to produce. Prophet Muhammad (S) teaches: "Never be lazy and helpless". There is no good in an individual who does not want to produce and earn money. And it is known that the unproductive hand is an unclean impure hand. Products should be useful and not harmful as defined in the Qur'an and the Islamic laws (Sharia).

Distribution

In its efforts to do away with classes in the society based on wealth and affluence, and reshaping it through distribution into an integrated society, Islam makes the following points:

- God owns wealth, power and natural resources. The individual or the institution is appointed by God as a trustee and custodian to manage them.

- Every being, human or not, has a minimum requirement to be able to live in dignity. This should be provided by the government to anyone who cannot meet his or her own needs.

• Islam respects private property and the right of ownership is protected.

• The system is paid back and balanced out through the act of *Zakah* (alms giving as an essential part of the system and faith). If this source is not enough, the Islamic government would apply a temporary tax on the rich and affluent to balance the budget as a religious duty (*Fard Kefaya*). *Zakah* is spent by the Islamic Government and distributed to the poor, the needy, the traveller (wayfarer), administrators and to help the oppressed indebtors to pay off their debts. Where Muslims live under a non-Islamic Government, Zakah must still be collected from the Muslims and spent for the good of society.

• The individuals are trained to feel socially responsible for others in the community. He/she cannot enjoy life while others cannot.

• The government is responsible for the basic needs of every citizen. These are food, shelter, clothing, education and health care.

• The only road to richness and to achievement is hard work and assumption of risk. It is not through inheritance. That is why Islamic law (by a detailed description in the Holy Qur'an Chapter 4) defines exactly how the estate is distributed after death. No one can make a will that attempts to alter the predefined distribution rates. In addition, if one wanted to include in his/her will a payout to others outside what the law requires, this is limited to a maximum of

1/3 of the total estate. This way money is always distributed and trickled down through the system every time it is accumulated, not through inheritance taxes to the government but through direct distribution to those who are entitled to it, hence reducing government and waste.

Consumption

Islam preaches moderation and a balanced pattern of consumption. Islam is a way of life. Over-consumption is condemned as the work of satan. Spending in the wrong way (bribery, illegal profits and/or reckless spending) and extravagant over-consumption of lawful matter are not allowed. Everyone is trained to plan for the future and to be careful. The story of prophet Joseph in the Holy Qur'an Chapter 12, is an important lesson in long-range planning.

BUSINESS ETHICS

Goals of the Business

• Maximize profits and services in a legal way to realize freedom and independence of the individual and the society using interdependence and interaction with other nations, communities and businesses. Islam promotes free markets and free international trade as the natural mechanism of getting people to know each other in order to promote peace and prosperity through communications, trading and mutual benefits.

• Develop new and improved ways and means to improve the quality of life and preserve the individual's most valuable asset, which is time. Time is life for a Muslim. Protection of the environment is a sacred duty of the Muslim.

• Focus on a long-term view of investing in the future without speculation, to provide long-term job opportunities for generations to come.

• Provide flexibility through strategic planning and training to prevent business cycles from negatively impacting the community, as we learn from the story of prophet Joseph in the Holy Qur'an (Chapter 12).

THE MARKET SYSTEM

• Markets should be free and open to everyone provided that other laws of the system are not violated.

• Information about products, goods and services should be made readily available, complete and known to all parties. Indeed, information is considered a part of the contract. Misrepresentations are punishable both in this life and in the hereafter. Full disclosure is a must.

• Monopoly and hoarding are strictly forbidden and prohibited.

• Prices are set on the basis of supply/demand using the auction open market system.

• Speculation in commodities is strictly forbidden. Markets are designed to bring a buyer (end user) and a seller (producer) together to consummate a deal. No speculation or interference with market forces of supply and demand is allowed.

MANAGEMENT ETHICS

• A manager is looked upon as a custodian on God's trust given to him/her to manage. He/she, on the other hand, is considered a shepherd of his/her employees. He/she provides guidance, vision and care for his/her subordinates to maximize their output, and keep the values of the religion and system intact. In fact prayers are part of the system, with the manager leading the prayer or at least pro-actively participating in it.

• A manager is chosen with strict qualifications:

> • Excellence in professionalism and knowledge

> • Performance and trust over time and piety

> • Good interpersonal relations as guided by the ultimate example of Prophet Mohammed (S) and all other prophets of God.

• A manager/owner of the work place is required to provide employees with maximum job security through continual training, through optimization and through community interrelationships.

MONEY AND FINANCE

BANKING AND INVESTMENT BANKING

• Money is not looked at as a commodity that commands a price, that is called interest as in the RIBA system. Money does not reproduce and give birth to money. Production and trading produce economic activity. Money is a means of transacting business and is used to measure the efficiency of doing business through the use of "rate of return on investment." Monetary policy is based on actual achievement of economic growth and productivity not on perceived future rates of growth, since the future is only known to God.

• Banks are required to operate on a 100% reserve basis; i.e. on an all cash transaction basis. If money is entrusted with a bank then it is a trust and should be returned intact as is. It also cannot be disposed of in the form of a facility to others without the consent of the owner. A service fee can be charged, however.

• Investment banks provide the role of bringing the owner of capital together with the owner of an idea or expertise to invest together and realize long-term economic growth. The investment bankers' role is education, evaluation, promotion and follow-up for the benefit of long-term growth not for a commission. The purpose is to realize the Islamic goal of making capital circulate within the community and to prevent the freezing of assets and capital. Islam prohibits trading paper instruments, speculation and manipulation. The objective is long-term investing.

Finally, there is one underlying holistic concept of producing income: *"Halal"* which means lawful and *"Haram"* which means unlawful.

VALUES TO ACHIEVE THE ISLAMIC BUSINESS ETHIC

PROFESSIONALISM

Professionalism is the talent of taking power through God, the source of all powers, to love what we do, to improve ourselves, to add to our experiences and to do the best we can at what we promised to do. Professionalism is making promises that can be delivered and, if possible, delivering them better than promised. Professionalism is Islam at work. It is the pride of doing what we know, the strength of being able to say "we do not know", when we do not, and the determination to try to learn more.

CONCENTRATION

Concentration is the ability to focus and listen. It speaks to you quietly above the roar of your mind. Concentration in prayers, in *Duaa* (supplication), in remembering God, and in our work trains us to ignore the extraneous, to dismiss the distractions, to avoid the pessimists and focuses at will. Concentration is part of *Ibada* (worship). It is clarity. It is what keeps our emotions from getting the better of us. Concentration keeps pressure from becoming paralysis, and keeps us away from diluting our efforts by spreading ourselves too thin.

Concentration is what keeps our eyes on our goals, allows us to turn reaction into action, disadvantage into opportunity and opportunity into success.

Our goals should be crystal clear. We need to build the foundation of a world-wide LARIBA Islamic financial system to bring the masses (*Alnas*) back to the basic values of trust, humbleness, sincerity and non-wasting through the LARIBA financial system.

CONSISTENCY

Consistency is unimpressed with a single success. Consistency confers medals only upon those who burn brightly with the repetition of achievement. It is more than a promise. It is performance over time. Consistency means never resting, never taking our talents, the gifts of God, for granted. Consistency is the practical proof that we are believers in God.

COMMITMENT

Commitment is what transforms a promise into reality. We need to promise God to build the financial infrastructure of our communities world-wide.

Commitment is the word that speaks of our intentions and the action which speaks louder than words. Commitment is making the time when there is none. Commitment is coming through time after time, year after year for the whole of our life.

Commitment is what character is made of. It is the power to change. It is the daily triumph of integrity, of belief in God, and belief in the future over skepticism.

CHAPTER THREE

REVIEW OF ISLAMIC ECONOMICS**

Over the last three decades, economics has received more attention from Muslim scholars and intellectuals than any other discipline. Islamic economics has matured as a discipline and "arrived." It has its own journal (*Journal of Research in Islamic Economics*), at least two research centers devoted to the subject and is now being taught in economics departments of numerous universities both in the Muslim world and in the West.

Prof. Muhammad Nejatullah Siddiqui's[1] highly praised survey of contemporary literature on the subject lists some 700 works in English, Arabic and Urdu. A more recent work by Muhammad Akram Khan[2] contains over 1500 citations. Islamic banks are mushrooming in almost every Muslim state, form Sudan to Iran, Pakistan, Bangladesh, Egypt and Malaysia. Many European cities have one or more Islamic banks. There is thus good reason to believe that Islamic economics has not only arrived, it is here to stay.

** *Based on a survey which appears in: Islamic Futures - The Shape of Ideas to Come, Ziauddin Sardar, Chap. 9 pp.198, Pelanduk Publications, Malaysia, 1988.*

DEFINITION OF ISLAMIC ECONOMICS

But what is Islamic economics? How does it differ from the conventional capitalist and socialist economic models? What are its axioms and principles? How will Islamic economics replace the dominant economic orders in Muslim societies? One of the first points emphasized by author after author is that Islamic economics is not capitalism minus interest plus zakah or socialism minus state control plus God. It is something unique and different and exclusive to Islam. How unique and how different is essentially the key issue.

S. M. Hasanuz Zaman[3] offers the following definition: "Islamic economics is the knowledge and application of injunctions and rules of the *Sharia* (Islamic Jurisprudence) that prevent injustice in the acquisition and disposal of material resources in order to provide satisfaction to human beings and enable them to perform their obligations to Allah (God) and society. M. Akram Khan[4] considered that "Islamic economics aims at the study of human *falah* (Salvation) achieved by organizing the resources of earth on the basis of cooperation and participation. The role of the *Sharia* (Islamic Jurisprudence), the notion of *adl* (justice) and *falah* (salvation), cooperation and sharing are central to Islamic economic philosophy of the total system of Islam." Siddiqui[2] sums up this philosophy as follows:

"The key to economic philosophy of Islam lies in man's relationship with God, His universe and His people, i.e. other human beings, and the nature and purpose of man's life on earth. Man-God relationship is defined by *Tawhid* (Oneness God). The essence of *Tawhid* is a total commitment to the will of Allah (God), involving both submission and mission to pattern human life in accordance with His will. The will of Allah (God) constitutes the source of value and becomes the end of human endeavour. Life on earth is a test, and its purpose should be to prove successful in the test by doing Allah's (God's) will. The entire universe with all the natural resources and powers is made amenable to exploitation by man, though it is owned by Allah (God) alone. Life on earth being a test and all the provisions available to man being in the nature of trust, man is accountable to Allah (God) and his success in the life hereafter depends on his performance in this life on earth."

But how is this economic *ibada* (worship) performed?

There are a host of Islamic concepts and values which define the extent and nature of economic activity. There are many positive values such as *iqtisad* (moderation), *adl* (justice), *ihsan* (kindness par excellence), *amanah* (honesty), *infaq* (spending to meet social obligations), *sabr* (patience) and *istislah* (public interest). Similarly, there are a number of values which are negative, and thus to be avoided: *zulm* (tyranny), *bukhl* (miserliness), *hirs* (greed), *iktinaz* (hoarding of wealth) and *israf* (extravagance). Economic activity within the positive parameters is halal (allowed and praiseworthy) and within the negetive parmeters is haram (prohibited and blameworthy) which has to be moderated. Production and distribution which are regulated by the halal-haram code must adhere to the notion of *adl* (justice). Collectively, these values and concepts, along with the main injunctions of the Qur'an, provide a framework for a unique, just and contemporary economic system.

THE CHALLENGE IS IN THE APPLICATION

Islamic concepts are almost always stated in theory. When it comes to the questions of "how it is to be done" and "what exactly needs to be done" problems emerge and differences arise. How can *Zakah* (the ritual of alms giving) be made the cornerstone of public finance in an Islamic society? How can brotherhood/sisterhood be promoted; and what needs to be done to ensure equity? How can wealth be redistributed? What needs to be done to ensure that wealth does not accumulate in fewer and fewer hands. What consumer goods constitute *israf* (extravagance)? What types of industry would lead to economic *zulm* (tyranny)? What types of technologies negate *adl* (justice) and promote *ihtikaar* (hoarding) of wealth? How can Islamic injunctions on the use of land be introduced without the use of force? What needs to be done to break the feudal structure in Muslim society and developing nations' society?

LARIBA ISLAMIC TERMINOLOGY, RIBA ANALYSIS

In the early sixties when Muslim economists were rediscovering the principles of Islamic economics, their output was in many respects genuinely original. The major subject they have tried to discuss is bank interest. They have played around bank interest, and have come sometimes very close to thinking that if they could avoid dealing with bank interest and introduce another modern means to provide the same motivation in a different way that could solve the problem. It was a huge attempt to cast Islamic institutions and dictates, like *Zakah* (the ritual of alms giving) and prohibition of interest, into RIBA economic mould. The dominant models guide the analysis and shape the inquiry: everything is compared and contrasted with capitalism and socialism, highlighting the fact that there is an underlying apologia at work.

Once the objectives of the LARIBA Islamic economics have been stated in terms of RIBA paradigm, it is a short step to accept the major institutions of the RIBA system and try to mould them into LARIBA Islamic shapes. The most obvious example of this is RIBA banking: the institution as it has evolved into the world since the industrial revolution has been accepted, without criticism and questions whether banks, as defined and developed over time, are really needed.

While the suggested alternative for interest, which is profit-sharing, reflects the true ideals of LARIBA of Islam, it cannot fit in an institution which has grown up solely on the basis of interest and RIBA.

Professor Siddiqui, describes the function of a banking system based on *"mudaraba"* *** as follows:[5]

*** *"Mudaraba" is a unique form of joint-venture capital transaction. According to Mudaraba an entity contributes all the capital and the other party contributes the expertise and/or labor. In return, both parties agree to share any realized profits. The owner of capital assumes any potential losses as part of the risk. The closest analog to this concept is a limited partnership agreement in the RIBA banking terminology.*

23

"A large number of depositors enter into individual *'mudaraba'* contracts with a banking company, organized on the basis of share capital, the contracts stipulating the sharing of the profits of the 'business of banking'. The bank undertakes two kinds of business. Firstly, it offers banking services for which the bank earns fees and commissions. Secondly, it assumes the role of a financier-entrepreneur making judicious selection of businessmen who seek capital from it, stipulating that they share with the profits of their productive enterprise. Liability to loss in a *'mudaraba'* contract attaches to the financier only, the working party i.e. the user of the capital bears no part of the loss accruing the capital extended by the financier. It follows that the loss incurred by an individual entrepreneur will be borne by the bank. Losses incurred on individual advances are likely to get absorbed by some of the profits accruing to the bank from the successful entrepreneurs. As long as the totality of profits accruing on banks' advances plus the fees and commissions earned by the bank remain a positive quantity, the depositors' capital and return on capital are safe. But what if the total earnings of the bank is a negative quantity? This will mean a loss, to be distributed equally on share capital and *'mudaraba'* deposits."

The central question is, should the ordinary act of depositing money become a risk-taking exercise. How can one plan for the future if one is not sure what will happen to one's money at the end of the financial year? And some of the Islamic LARIBA banks as they are normally defined have no guarantee that they will get a return on their investments. Consider what will happen to a rural agricultural bank in a year of bad harvest when it has invested all its capital in the labor of the local farmers! If the financier is risking his/her capital, he/she is likely to demand a hefty share of the profit; so the poor entrepreneur ends up working for the bank instead of him/herself. And if the bank does not ask for a lion's share of the profit, how can it ensure that it covers for all those entrepreneurs who have lost its money? Perhaps both the bank and the entrepreneur are getting a bad deal. Perhaps this is why many of the Islamic banks are losing their investments so rapidly.

The point of this valid and justified criticism is not that the principles of *"mudaraba"* do not work, but that the RIBA institution of banking is the wrong place to put an Islamic injunction into practice. Moreover, RIBA economic institutions do not come on their own: they bring the entire system with them. Banking, as Alvin Toffler[6] points out so powerfully in his book "Third Wave," is the central institution of the modern money system. Accept the RIBA banks and you accept the entire RIBA economic monetary and financial structure and theoretical framework that comes with it. The two are integrated and cannot be decoupled.

The abolition of RIBA and the collection of *Zakah* are the cornerstones of the LARIBA economic system. But the natural emphasis of a system that outlaws RIBA interest would be to play down the role of money, not to raise it as the arch factor of the economy.

THE ROLE OF MONEY IN RIBA BANKING SYSTEM

Many economists and individuals are hypnotized by money, and look only at those sectors of production and consumption that are monetized and involve cash

25

transactions. The emphasis on the monetized economy has meant that Islamic economics has equated the monetized sectors of a country with the whole system of production, consumption and maintenance.

SUGGESTED SOLUTIONS TOWARDS A LARIBA SYSTEM

A study by Umar Chapra[7] on Islamic banking and monetary system, suggests a package of reforms which includes moderation in spending, elimination of hoarding, efficient use of savings, responsible government spending, increase in equity financing, reducing the powers of banks, and establishment of "sane" stock markets. In addition, the following institutions were suggested: 1. a central bank, 2. commercial banks, 3. non-bank financial institutions, 4. specialized credit institutions, 5. deposit insurance corporations, and 6. investment audit corporation. Once this institutional set-up has emerged, a step-by-step transition can be undertaken to an interest-free economy. The transition involves the declaration of interest as illegal, substantial increases in equity/loan ratio of Muslim countries and communities, reform of the tax system, mobilization of idle funds, and the gradual conversion of interest RIBA-oriented financial institutions into profit-sharing ones. Chapra[7] clearly believes that an important step towards a just society can be produced simply by modifying the monetary system.

Additional emphasis should be directed to the relationship between production and consumption, the role or mode of production in shaping a society, the psychological impact of the divorce — in time, space and social distance — between a producer and a consumer and the illusionary nature of paper money." What is the role of theory of profit in Islam?" "What function does macro consumption perform in Islamic economics?"

Many Muslim economists have based their analysis on a number of metaphysical assumptions: first, that money is to be studied like a physical commodity; second, what needs to be done is to analyze how the money system of today actually works; third, that monetary problems can be solved by modifying the dominant institutions of RIBA; fourth, that the tools of modern economics, whose cultural impact needs to be appreciated by Muslim economists, can solve the problem of Islamic LARIBA economics; fifth, that the economic environment is never depleted; and sixth that the goals of the Islamic LARIBA economic system can be achieved without changing the energy base of Muslim countries.

Many Muslim economists need to focus on working on research directed toward producing policies that are different from the capitalist and socialist alternatives. If this is not done, Muslim countries will end up with the same crisis that confronts industrialized societies.

THE AXIOMATIC ANALYSIS

If Islamic LARIBA economics, just like Islamic science, has any meaning it is purely in the context of Islamic society and Muslim civilization. In this context, Islamic LARIBA economics has to rely not just on Islamic principles and injunctions, but must develop its own tools of thought and analysis and its unique institutions and apply such on Muslim communities. Islamic LARIBA economic institutions have to be rediscovered, evolved and invented on the basis of the needs of Muslim societies and the principles of Islam, not taken or adopted from what already exists in the market-place. This means that Islamic LARIBA economics must construct a living dynamic Islamic economic system, concept by concept, institution by institution, applying Islamic junctions such as the prohibition of RIBA and introduction of Zakah in a truly authentic manner.

More recently, however, Syed Nawab Haider Naqvi[8] in his "Ethics and Economics: An Islamic Synthesis" argues that any set of axioms to be meaningful must satisfy four criteria: they must be adequate and legitimate representations of Islam's ethical views; they must form the smallest possible set; the elements of the set must be internally consistent; and the axioms must have predictive powers. Four axioms: unity, equilibrium, free will and responsibility were recommended. Unity, or Tawhid, refers not only to the unity of God, but also the unity of human life and the healing of the "current schism between ethics and economics." Social justice is only one component of equilibrium which is derived from adl (justice). Free will refers to human freedom in the

28

realm on worldly affairs; but free will can also lead to the denial of unity and upset nature's equilibrium unless man is made responsible for his/her actions. All four concepts are interlinked and interrelated, and cannot be isolated from each other. Naqvi[8] uses his four axioms to develop the basic policy objectives of the Islamic LARIBA economic system. He isolates social justice, universal education, economic growth and employment generation as the key policy objectives of Islamic LARIBA economics.

Language and concepts have a profound impact on our thinking. *Tawhid* (unity), *adl* (justice), *istislah* (public interest) and *khilafah* (leadership as a vicegerent of God on earth), are all examples of the rich reservoir of concepts to be found in the Qur'an and Sunnah (the traditions and teachings of Prophet Muhammad (S)). It is believed that they are not there to be ignored. How does one, for example, on the basis of linear logic, reconcile the idea that *Zakah,* which involves subtracting from one's income, can actually lead to increase of wealth? Growth by subtraction is an idea that RIBA economics has no understanding of.

The linear logic of RIBA economics is reflected in the present structure of the world. Economically and technologically, the globe is structured as though developing countries, including all Muslim countries, were colonies of the industrialized states. Colonialism is alive and well, and many industrialized countries are reaping its benefits.

It is believed that Islamic LARIBA economics is not going to break this structure if it freely borrows from this paradigm. On the contrary, it may become part of the structure. Thus, all those Muslim economists who argue that we should not hesitate to borrow the "good " and "neutral" bits of the RIBA economic theory may be asking to be absorbed into the dominant paradigm. The fact is that RIBA economics is one vast, interlinked, value-laden, self-perpetuating system that is taking linear logic to its ultimate conclusion.

If Islamic LARIBA economics is to move toward the ideals, then it must develop not just its own body of theories and models, but also its own tools and modes of logic, thought and actual physical operation. It must assume a civilizational role and work towards laying the foundations and building the structures of a Muslim civilization of the future. It has to break the shell of an atomized discipline and become a multi-disciplinary mode of inquiry, taking into consideration the social organizations, the political ideals, the environmental imperatives, and scientific and technological needs of Muslim underdeveloped societies.

Economics has to draw not just from Muslim history, and contemporary Muslim societies, but also from a clear vision about the future. Islamic economics has to develop a future consciousness for the Muslims and the society at large.

The following are global trends that spell danger for Muslim countries and the world and should be taken in consideration:

1. The world is shrinking and becoming more and more economically interlinked and interdependent. The only winners are the RIBA banking systems. How to co-exist with and/or delink from the world's economic and monetary systems must, therefore, become a major theme of Islamic LARIBA economics.

2. Electronic banking and funds transfer systems are giving money an unparalleled and dangerous importance. Because of the speed of electronic systems, the same amount of money now is estimated to support five times as many transactions as before. Thus the speeding up of money handling also increases its velocity of circulation. At a point not too distant in the future, when the speed of transaction reaches "real time," money will acquire a strange new status. The velocity of the information about money flows would lose all relationship with thermodynamic realities of the actual system (subject to natural cycles of crops, weather, friction, inertia, and human frailties), and the amount of money and capital available at any point in the banking system would tend towards infinity. As information about the money system become delinked from actual events, all manner of new ventures and schemes might be initiated by false promissory notes signaling capital availability with nothing more than an electronic impulse over a computer terminal.

Moreover, computerization of stock markets throughout the world has blurred the distinction between investment and speculation. The entire system is moving towards becoming a huge worldwide gambling casino with no pretension to serving social needs. Muslim LARIBA economists must be aware of the changing role of money and its implications for Muslim societies. They must work to diversify the basis of Islamic LARIBA economic thought towards non-monetarist and non-fiscal areas.

3. Information itself is becoming a key commodity. Economic power in the future will be determined by the ability to

generate and having access to information. It will play the same role as energy is playing now. Thus, Islamic LARIBA economic theory must be developed to cope with non-material commodities like information.

4. The use of energy and other natural resources (especially water) of a society is intrinsically tied with economics. The globe's energy and natural resources are depleting at a rapid rate. Both inflation and employment are tied to the rate of depletion of energy and natural resources. As it becomes more costly to extract energy and other natural resources, they become more and more scarce, so the cost of transforming them into usable commodities increases. Throughout the world, the price of basic goods and services is tied to the costs associated with the extraction and transformation of energy. Unemployment is the other side of the equation: the faster conventional sources of energy run out, more and more people become unemployed and underemployed. Thus transformation to a renewable energy base is essential for the future survival of the world.

5. At present, Muslim and other developing countries are essentially consumer states relying exclusively on imported goods. This situation is likely to get worse and the associated ill-effects of the ever-increasing social, psychological and intellectual distance between producers and consumers will multiply at greater speeds. A major task of Islamic LARIBA economics is to change the patterns of consumption in Muslim societies as well as to direct production towards directions which are more suitable to the needs of Muslim consumer. The formidable task is to transform these ethics into a dynamic economic system that has its individual identity with its own institutions and methodological tools. This system will provide a viable,

kinder and gentler alternative to the dominant systems of RIBA economies.

6. Muslim LARIBA economists, social scientists and leaders living outside the Muslim countries in many of the developed countries of world must carve a role for themselves to implement the theory of Islamic LARIBA financing in their communities in the world and try to branch out into the Muslim and developing countries world-wide in order to facilitate the bringing about of the dream of a world-wide community based LARIBA financing system.

CHAPTER FOUR

THE CHALLENGE

STARTING A LARIBA BANK
IN A RIBA BANKING WORLD

We need to clearly differentiate between two important approaches to the start-up of a "LARIBA" bank. These are:

1. The establishment of a "LARIBA" bank within a master plan of a perfect Muslim society which is governed by a dedicated Islamic government and operates by a full fledged and complete Islamic LARIBA financial system, and

2. The establishment of a "LARIBA" bank which follows the Islamic LARIBA laws and which is independent of the other parts of the society at large, in a society which does not operate according to the Islamic laws. This approach

assumes that the transformation to a full Islamic society governed by Islamic laws and ethics will take time.

The first approach will result in applying the prohibition of RIBA in the banking system in its totality. Yet, in the second approach, the prohibition of RIBA will be applied only to the particular LARIBA bank.

We all live in this second option. In fact, regardless of whether a government is in a Muslim land, or non-Muslim land, most everyone, with a very few exceptions, does not apply Islamic laws in their entirety.

That is why one needs to find a format that is legally acceptable from the point of view of Islamic law in our efforts to establish an Islamic LARIBA bank in a world which is not governed, in most cases, by Islamic laws. The following three conditions are thought to be necessary and required to achieve our goal:

1.   The LARIBA bank should not violate the rules and laws of Islamic LARIBA banking and financing and the spirit of LARIBA Islamic economic principles.

2.   The LARIBA bank should operate and compete in all aspects of the banking business with the other RIBA banking institutions in the community. The LARIBA bank should be designed to have the flexibility, operating

creativity and the financial products "manufacturing" ability to attract customers (Muslims and non-Muslims) and to keep them. It should aspire to make a clear and distinguished difference in the lives of the citizens of the community at large.

3. The LARIBA bank should be operated as a profitable business entity. In particular, the LARIBA bank should offer superior services and returns as compared to the RIBA banks. In addition, the LARIBA bank should play an important role which is felt by the community at all levels, especially at the grass roots level. The LARIBA bank in its active effort to serve the community will become the force behind capital accumulation from the community and in using that capital to finance projects and services which will make a difference in the economic well-being of the community. This is done through job creation for members of the community and others outside the community.

4. The LARIBA bank should be more sensitive to risk management than the RIBA banks. So, in its efforts of capital accumulation, the LARIBA bank, in its slow and gradual effort to get established, should target a smaller percentage of the assets and savings of the community to be used in LARIBA financing. It should also be made clear to the participating investors, that

because of the start-up nature of the LARIBA bank venture, there is a risk of losing all or part of their assets. But on the other hand, it should be made clear both operationally and to the investors that the bank will apply careful due diligence and portfolio diversification methods and will keep enough reserves for potential losses in order to minimize the possibility of losing money while paying acceptable returns on the investment.

5.   The LARIBA bank should start by a core group of shareholders who believe in the dream of having a bank and/or a finance company which operates according to the LARIBA system. They should satisfy the following requirements:

5.1   They should be hand picked to form a homogeneous group with the same vision, dreams, social and personal backgrounds as well as the same investment and business temperament.

5.2.   They should be financially well-to-do (but not necessarily very rich). This will make them able to meet any run on the LARIBA bank in case a rumor or an unexpected event occurs.This way the LARIBA bank will always be able to meet any requests for withdrawal of investors' deposits:

5.3. They should come with a highly diversified actual "hands-on" experience in the business fields to be targeted for financing by the LARIBA bank. This way, the bank will be able to evaluate the projects by owners/experts who are looked upon as managing their own funds and who are in actual operational sense the "managing partners" (not employees) of the LARIBA bank.

5.4. They should be willing to accept no pay or low pay for their services to reduce the overhead expenses of the LARIBA bank, especially when the LARIBA bank is in its infancy and the assets under management are still small.

6. The LARIBA bank should structure its capital such that the core group of shareholders' capital and/or investments represent at least 50% of the total assets under management. This way the LARIBA bank can meet any unexpected run on its deposits. (As mentioned above under 5.2)

7. Deposited (investors') assets in the LARIBA bank are looked upon as liabilities of the shareholders. This way every shareholder/member of the board of directors and bank management will make sure to carefully evaluate every project to be financed by the LARIBA bank to minimize their perceived personal liability.

8. Investments made by the LARIBA bank should be shorter term in the beginning (3-5 years) to assure enough cash flow to meet any demands for withdrawals by investors.

SECTION II

Historic Review and Details of
The Modern Monetary System and the
European Monetary Union

This section summarizes the history of developing the most sophisticated monetary system in the world; i.e. the American monetary system, and the policies of the U.S. Federal Reserve Board to manage the economy in the U.S. through monetary adjustments and interest rates on the U.S. Dollar. Chapter 5 reviews the historic development of the system, and the concept of creation of credit in the banking system.

In an effort to shed some light on the effect of monetary policy on inflation and the use of monetary policy to enhance major political goals, a case study on the post World War II international monetary system is reviewed in chapter 6. Chapter 7 reviews Europe's efforts to unite as a case study for all these nations with homogeneous and converging social and human values and with integrated market and economic potentials on their way to realize the same dream of unity as that of Europe.

CHAPTER FIVE

THE FEDERAL RESERVE SYSTEM
OF THE UNITED STATES****

The U.S. dollar has become the leading reserve currency of the world. Any discussion of financial and monetary system, especially regarding the LARIBA system as compared to the RIBA system, should be based on a clear understanding of how the U.S. Dollar monetary policies are handled. It is a known fact that most world currencies are either directly pegged to the U.S. dollar or are dependent on the U.S. dollar. **This chapter is a must for everyone who has the dream of building a LARIBA banking system.**

In an effort to stabilize the U.S. monetary element of the economy and to systemize the process of money and credit creation, the U.S. developed one of the most sophisticated central bank systems in the world. The system is considered to be one of the most important pillars upon which the U.S.

****   *Based on: David H. Friedman, Essentials of Banking, American Bankers Association, 1989.*

as a whole is built. The following is a summary of how the system was developed, where it derives its power from and how it operates.

MONEY CREATION IN THE U.S.
THE FEDERAL RESERVE SYSTEM

AMERICAN CURRENCY PROBLEMS BEFORE
CREATION OF THE FEDERAL RESERVE

The small quantity of paper currency that circulated in the United States' early years consisted of the notes issued by the First (1791) and Second (1816) Banks of the United States—two precursors of the Federal Reserve. After the Second Bank of the United States closed in 1836, the dominant form of currency became private bank notes issued by state-chartered commercial banks (normally redeemable on demand for gold or silver).

The U.S. did not have a uniform national currency, and the system of state-bank issues of notes was confusing and inefficient. By the 1860s, as many as 8,000 different issues of state bank notes were circulating in the United States. Banks rarely accepted at face value notes issued by banks unknown to them.

During the Civil War national bank notes were issued, and until 1913 these formed the bulk of the nation's paper currency. National bank notes were currency the government gave to nationally chartered commercial banks for them to issue as their own. National bank notes grew out of the government's need to raise money to finance the Union army. Faced with a depleted treasury and reluctant to raise taxes on northern industry, President Lincoln reluctantly agreed to a plan formulated by his Secretary of Treasury, Salmon Chase. Under Chase's plan, the federal government would offer a new type of banking license—a federal, or national, charter. A bank with a national charter would have the power to issue a new form of currency; national bank notes. However, for each note issued, the bank would have to hold a somewhat larger dollar value of government securities as collateral (a "backing" requirement). The banks could purchase the government securities directly from the Treasury for gold and silver; a universally accepted money at that time. In effect, the government would receive money assets (gold and silver) in return for its liabilities (government securities). Chase's plan was embodied in the National Banking Act of 1863.

To enhance the prospect that national bank notes would be successful and to eliminate the competition from notes issued by state banks, Chase also developed a tax that Congress gradually increased until the state bank practice of issuing currency ended.

Because national bank notes had to be fully collateralized government securities, the nation's supply of paper currency effectively depended on the government's debt. The supply of currency expanded and contracted in direct response to changes in the value of government securities in the nation's bond markets and not in response to the needs of the economy. When the government began repaying its Civil War debt, redeeming and retiring securities issued in earlier years, the supply of collateral available in the banking system for note issuance shrank. The supply of currency was inelastic (incapable of adjusting to the public's changing needs and demands), and this led to the money panics (episodes of irrational public hoarding and runs on banks) that periodically plagued the economy of U.S.A.

THE PYRAMID OF BANK RESERVES

The National Banking Act of 1863 specified three tiers of reserve requirements for national banks. Small "country" banks could keep some of their reserves in cash but were required to deposit most of their reserves with the larger "Reserve City" banks (those in the nation's major cities). Reserve City banks had to deposit most of their own reserves in still larger "Central Reserve City" banks (those in the nation's money centers of New York, Chicago, and St. Louis). The central reserve city banks had to keep all their reserves in vault cash.

The banking system's reserves were thus effectively dispersed throughout the country and could not be quickly transferred to banks in regions that might be under liquidity pressure. Because the central reserve city banks were the ultimate depositories of the banking systems' reserves, they were particularly susceptible to the accumulation of pressures that often led to bank panics.

A bank panic would generally begin in the Midwest, when small banks found they did not have enough currency on hand to pay out to farmers. These banks would call on their reserve city correspondents for their reserves. The reserve city correspondents, in turn, would call on the central reserve city banks for their reserves. Thus, a few central reserve city banks were often hit by the cumulative shock to liquidity that the needs of thousands of country banks generated. **A fundamental problem was lack of a <u>lender of last resort</u> for the banking system; a source of guaranteed liquidity that all banks could tap when they needed money.**

THE FEDERAL RESERVE BOARD OF THE UNITED STATES OF AMERICA

The Federal Reserve power is derived from the U.S. Constitution (Article I, Section 8). The article states: "Congress shall have power ... to coin money (and) regulate the value thereof...." The Federal Reserve Act of 1913 established the Federal Reserve to realize the following objectives:

1. Furnish an elastic currency which responds to the economic needs of the nation.

2. Serve as a last resort to defend against any run on the banking system of the nations.

3. Establish a more effective and responsive system to supervise banks.

4. Improve the efficiency of the national payment mechanism.

The 1946 Employment Act established the following national goals:

1. Full employment.

2. Price stability.

3. Economic growth.

These goals were expanded in 1978 when the Congress passed the Full Employment and Balanced Growth Act. These are the expanded goals:

1. Full employment.

2. Increased real income (net of inflation).

3. Balanced economic growth.

4. Balanced federal budget.

5. Growth in productivity.

6. Improved balance of trade.

7. Price stability.

The Act also required the Federal Reserve to report to the Congress twice a year on its monetary policies as they relate to the goals outlined in the 1978 Full Employment and Balanced Growth Acts.

FUNCTIONS OF THE FEDERAL RESERVE

The three basic functions of the Federal Reserve are:

1. Implementation of Monetary Policy:

> This is done through the use of three primary control devices which are:

> 1.1. Setting the reserve requirements of the banks.

> 1.2. Setting the discount rate at which the Federal Reserve lends the banks.

> 1.3. Setting the monetary growth or contraction through the activities of the Federal Open Market Committee (FOMC). The monetary expansion or contraction is done through the purchase or selling of Government securities respectively.

2. Providing Payment Services for the Depositories:

> Like loans, check collections, currency insurance, wire transfers, and account settlements.

3. Serving as a Bank for the Federal Government:

> 3.1. Responsible for supervising and regulating banks.
> 3.2. Keeps U.S. Federal Government checking account.

3.3. Sells and redeems interest payment on U.S. Government securities.

3.4. Establishes relations with foreign central banks and foreign exchange trading world-wide.

The Federal Reserve was made as an independent branch of the politics of governing. The U.S. monetary policy, which includes adjusting interest rate and money supply, is designed and implemented without any political interference from the President or the Congress. In such a unique set up, the monetary policy would be implemented for the interest of the nation and not to promote a certain political party, the Congress or the President. On the other hand, the President of the United States and the Congress decide on the fiscal policy of the Government which includes the federal budget, taxes and government spending. The Federal Reserve structure as an independent central bank is unique among the world's central banks. This adds to the power of the Federal Reserve to influence the U.S. economy and to bring creditability to the U.S. Dollar world-wide.

Structure of the Federal Reserve

The structure of the Federal Reserve is unique among the world's central banks. It consists of:

- A presidentially appointed Board of Governors with general responsibilities for oversight,

- Twelve regional Federal Reserve banks that are private institutions nominally owned by their stockholders (commercial banks that are members of the Federal Reserve System), and

- The Federal Open Market Committee (FOMC). The committee is composed of a 12-member policy making committee of the Federal Reserve. The 12 members consist of the 7 governors appointed by the President and 5 regional reserve bank presidents. The nation's monetary policy is decided at the monthly meetings of the FOMC.

The Federal Reserve banks are directed by nine-member boards of directors. Congress again stipulated a unique structure for those boards to insure that the selection process does not favor bankers and allow them to become a majority on any given Federal Reserve bank board. The Congress, in doing so, wanted to ensure that the views and concerns of all economic interest groups would be expressed and heard during the development of monetary policy. The nine-member board of directors of a Federal Reserve bank is elected as follows:

1. Member commercial banks elect 3 members from the banking community and 3 members from agricultural, commercial, industrial, services, labor, and consumer communities.

2. The Federal Reserve Board of Governors appoints 3 directors on its own. It also appoints the Reserve banks' presidents.

For a detailed description of the operation of the Federal Reserve and the process used to adjust and manage interest rates please read David H. Fridman, *Essential of Banking*, American Bankers Associations 1989.

The above discussion clearly indicates that interest rates especially related to the U.S. dollar are reflections of the way the Federal Reserve Board manages its monetary policy in response to many other factors. Hence, the real intention of this section. It is hoped that those who translate LARIBA banking as interest free banking would understand that LARIBA banking is much deeper in goal and fundamentally different at heart from just waiving the word "interest" away.

CREATION OF CREDIT AND THE MONEY MULTIPLIER OF THE U.S. BANKING SYSTEM

"T" ACCOUNT TRACKING OF ONE LOAN MADE BY A BANK AND THE MULTIPLE DEPOSITS IT GENERATES

"T" accounts are abstracts of a bank's balance sheet that show only the changes in the bank's assets and liabilities. For the sake of simplicity, assume, in this T-account example, that

• All the deposits created by banks stay in the banking system.

• Demand deposits are the only form in which newly created funds are held.

• Banks lend out every available dollar.

These assumptions do not by any means reflect reality. Some deposits created by banks leak out of the banking system into non-bank financial institutions and money market instruments. Consumers and businesses typically convert some newly acquired demand deposits into cash. Banks do not usually lend (or invest) every available dollar not because they do not want to, but because the pace with which deposits flow in and out of banks on any given day is often so rapid and the volume so large, and the net effect of check collections so uncertain, that only at the end of the day do banks know just how much net funds they have to support new loans.

Nonetheless, these assumptions, abstract as they may be, do not distort the fundamental process by which banks create deposits, which takes place in the following sequence of steps:

1. Assume that Bank A receives a cash deposit of $10,000 from a customer for credit to the customer's transaction account. Under Federal Reserve requirements, the bank must hold an amount of reserves—vault cash or deposit balances at a Federal Reserve bank—equal to a fixed percentage of its deposits; assume 10 percent. Thus, Bank A must hold $1,000 in required reserves against its new $10,000 deposit and has $9,000 in excess reserves. These excess reserves can support a new $9,000 loan and the creation of $9,000 in demand deposits entailed by such a loan.

BANK A

Assets		Liabilities	
Cash Assets	$10,000*	Demand Deposits	$10,000
		Demand Deposits created for	
New Loans	$9,000	borrowing	$ 9,000

* Required reserves $1,000 (10% of deposits)

2. When Bank A makes the loan, both its assets and its liabilities will temporarily increase to $19,000, reflecting the addition of the loan to its earning assets portfolio and the addition of the newly created demand deposit to its total liabilities. However, as soon as the borrower uses the newly created funds, Bank A's assets and liabilities will decline to their pre-loan level as an inevitable result of the check collection process.

3. Assume that the borrower writes a check for the loan amount to a manufacturing company that has an account at Bank B. When the borrower's $9,000 check clears, bank A will have to transfer $9,000 of its cash assets in payment for the check to the presenting bank (Bank B). Bank A will also strike the $9,000 demand deposit liability carried for the borrower from its books. Thus, after check clearance, Bank A has $10,000 in assets and $10,000 in liabilities. Note, however, that the composition of its assets has changed. Before the loan, it had $10,000 in cash assets, now it has $1,000 in cash assets and $9,000 in loan assets. The $1,000 in cash assets meets the assumed 10 percent reserve requirement ratio against transaction account liabilities.

	BANK A		BANK B

Assets	**Liabilities**	**Assets**	**Liabilities**
Cash Assets $1,000 Loan $9,000	Demand Deposit $10,000	Cash Assets $9,000a	Demand Deposit $9,000

a. Required reserves $ 900
Excess reserves $8,100

4. The $9,000 in deposit created by Bank A is now a demand deposit on the books of Bank B, increasing that bank's liabilities. However, Bank B also received a transfer of $9,000 in cash assets when it received payment for the check deposited by the manufacturing company. Bank B, subject to the same 10 percent reserve requirement as Bank A, must keep $900 against the deposit but can use the remaining $8,100 to support a new loan and the creation of a new $8,100 deposit.

5. When Bank B makes the $8,100 loan its assets and liabilities will increase initially and then decline to their pre-loan level in response to the collection of the borrower's check. Assume that the borrower writes a check for the loan amount to pay for a corporate service and that the corporation deposits the check in its account in Bank C. Bank B's newly created $8,100 will now reside as a liability in Bank C, together with the $8,100 in cash assets Bank B had to transfer in payment for the check.

	BANK B		BANK C
Assets	**Liabilities**	**Assets**	**Liabilities**
Cash Assets $ 900 Loan $8,100	Demand Deposit $ 9,000	Cash Assets $8,100a	Demand Deposit $8,100

a. Required reserves $ 810
Excess reserves $7,290

6. Bank C, in turn, will now be able to create demand deposits equal to 90 percent of its new cash assets. If it does so it will give still another bank the ability to create new deposits.

In theory, this process of bank deposit creation can continue through hundreds of banks, generating, in this example, a total amount of deposits on all banks' books 10 times greater than the $10,000 in cash deposits that started the process. The "multiplier," or expansion coefficient, is the reciprocal of the reserve requirement ratio. In this example, because the reserve requirement ratio is 10 percent, the multiplier is 10. This simple multiplier is valid only in the context of this example. In the real world of banking there are separate reserve requirements for different types and amounts of liabilities. This multiple expansion of bank-created deposits is characteristic of banking systems but not of individual banks. No bank can create deposits in any amount greater than its excess reserves. If it did, it would find itself in a reserve deficiency as soon as the borrower's check cleared. This act violates the Federal Reserve rules and the bank will be subject to severel federal stipulations, controls and penalties.

CHAPTER SIX

THE POST WORLD WAR II INTERNATIONAL MONETARY SYSTEM

The Bretton Woods System

After World War II, the Western allies led by the U.S.A. met in Bretton Woods in 1944 to agree on an international monetary system. The International Monetary Fund (IMF) was established by the Bretton Woods Agreement.

The Agreement foresaw the need for occasional adjustments in exchange rates among the various currencies of the Western allies. At the time, this was thought to be a seldom used and highly exceptional emergency operation that most nations, and especially the industrialized nations, would not have to resort to.

To deal with the expected post World War II growth in international economic and trade activities, and to facilitate it, a set of rules was laid down at an international monetary conference in July 1944. This is the well known Bretton Woods Agreement, which led to the creation of the International Monetary Fund, or IMF. Among the stated objectives of the IMF are the following:

1. Expansion and balanced growth of international trade.

2. Promotion of exchange rate stability among international currencies, and

3. Shortening the duration and lessening the degree of disequilibrium in the international balances of payments of member countries.

So far, the only one objective that was met was the growth of international trade.

The Balance of Payment Concept

The U.S. experiences a balance-of-payment deficit when more U.S. dollars leave the country than enter it. Dollars leave the country when Americans buy goods and services abroad (import) or when they invest abroad.

Conversely, dollars enter the country when foreigners buy U.S.-made goods and services, or when foreigners invest here in the U.S.

These are not the only causes of international dollar flows, but they are the major ones. Others are such as international remittances, military and non-military grants, international aid, etc.

The Bretton Woods Agreement worked reasonably well in the first few years of its existence, perhaps because the IMF, being in its infancy, moved with caution. By 1950, the first signs of trouble started to appear. From then on, the United States persisted in accumulating balance-of-payment deficits, with only rare and insignificant exceptions. The question is, how did the U.S. get away with this persistent deficit accumulation for so long when no other nation could? The simple answer: By convincing the creditor nations to hold the U.S. dollar itself as a means of settling its deficit.

As the U.S. dollar continued to accumulate in foreign central banks, it was always thought that a simple reversal of policies could, in due time, reverse the trend. In the meantime, as long as the U.S. government adhered to its policy of keeping its dollar pegged to gold and convertible into gold, a run on the U.S. gold stock was not likely. If a run on gold were to be made, the U.S. would lose. But so would most Western nations, since they would be left holding U.S. monetary units for which there was no gold backing.

As it became increasingly clear with time, the Bretton Woods Agreement allowed the U.S. to assume the role of the monopolistic money-supplier to the world. The purchase mechanism provided the U.S. with foreign-made goods and/or services. The loan mechanism (compounded by the Euro-and Asia-dollar markets) allowed the U.S. corporations to make capital investments abroad; i.e. to buy up foreign companies and productive facilities or to create such facilities on foreign soil. **In return for this, the U.S. had to run the money printing presses a little faster.**

The only way America could make U.S. dollars available to the outside world was by incurring balance-of-payments deficit. The greater the deficit, the greater the international liquidity. The world got hooked on the spend, spend and spend policies to meet their ever increasing consumptive behavior and localized war adventures. These activities were financed indirectly through America by using the U.S. dollar as the reserve currency of the world through the IMF.

The perception of the Western allies that the pre-1971 International Monetary System favored the United States was not the only area of friction among the leading nations of the West. Money, at least the so called M1-concept, is defined as: all checking account deposits and currency in the hands of the U.S. non-bank public. This part of the total money aggregate created by the Fed is watched closely by them to make sure that the economy is under control. But since the U.S. dollars held outside the U.S., either privately or by foreign central banks, do not fall in the M1-category, the Fed did not concern itself with the supply of dollars held abroad.

As an example, suppose the U.S. M1 money supply is $500 billion and that some $50 billion (only 10%) wind up abroad. That would leave $450 billion at home here in the U.S.; not enough to sustain the growth of the economy (Gross National Product-GNP) at the previous level of $500 billion, since the reduction in money supply to the public de-stimulates and reduces the nation's public demand (to buy goods and services). So, America has what looks like a demand-induced recession on its hands. To keep the economy going in the U.S., the Federal Reserve in this case, will count and recount the M1-(domestic) money supply, find it short $50 billion and promptly fill the gap (that was during the 60's and 70's; now the Fed watches the M2-supply which includes large CD's and the M3-supply which include Euro-dollar term deposits and large deposits and money market accounts). This supposedly would solve the problem and bring back demand. The GNP would rise, unemployment is reduced and the problem is solved.

The question is: is it really solved? More to the point: if America is short $50 billion, where did the money go? And what is its impact at the new locations overseas? The answer: **It went abroad and caused inflationary pressures there.**

In summary, by not filling the money gap created by transfer of dollars abroad, a recession is generated in the U.S. and on the other hand, by filling the gap, a U.S. recession is averted but inflation is created abroad. What would be the choice for the Fed? The lesser of the two evils: inflate abroad.

MR. NIXON ABANDONS
THE U.S. DOLLAR/GOLD PARITY

In 1971, many European officials started realizing what was happening and they screamed foul. Mr. Spiro Agnew (then the Vice President of the U.S.), the late Mr. John Connally (then the U.S. Secretary of the Treasury), and Mr. George Schultz (then the Director of the U.S. Office of Management and Budget, OMB, and later Mr. Reagan's Secretary of State and former chairman of Bechtel Corp.) all refused to address the problem of balancing the U.S. balance of payments. In short, America refused to take action. The dollar continued to accumulate abroad, and the inevitable finally took place. During the second week of August 1971, another run on the U.S. gold reserves was stopped by President Nixon. On August 15, 1971, Mr. Nixon suspended the backbone of the Bretton Woods Agreement. He declared the suspension of the convertability of the U.S. dollar into gold.

There had been previous attacks on the U.S. dollar. In 1965, France under President Charles de Gaulle, converted just under $1 billion into gold. In 1968, the dollar was attacked again. The "two-tier" gold market was then created as an emergency measure. The U.S. no longer stood ready to exchange an ounce of gold for $35 (as per the Bretton Woods Agreement) to just anyone. Only foreign governments and/or central banks were qualified for the trade. **At that time the U.S. cut itself loose from the private international gold market, just as it has abandoned and outlawed the private domestic gold market in 1933.** The trouble was that when that gate was shut, a small back door was left open. Under the existing IMF rules at the time, member governments (except Switzerland) were obliged never to let their currency money-parity deviate by more than 1% up or down from the IMF set fixed exchange rate relative to the U.S. dollar. Germany, in particular, was prohibited, by agreement, to let the price of the U.S. dollar fall. The only option available to the Deutsche Bank (Germany's Central Bank, which always stood as politically independent and with a clear mandate to fight inflation) was to buy U.S. dollars at the fixed exchange rate to support the fixed exchange rate agreed upon by the IMF agreement.

The net result was expected. The U.S. dollars were in the

hands of foreign central banks. In the days preceding President Nixon's new economic policy, that meant: **That these foreign central banks had access to Fort Knox's gold through exchanging that gold for U.S. Dollars as the Bretton Woods Agreement stipulated.** At the time, the foreign central banks of major European countries (many of them with American troops in some sort on their soils) were assumed to be reasonable institutions that would not make a run on the U.S. gold.

In early May 1971, such a private attack on the U.S. dollar forced four countries; namely Germany, Holland, Belgium and Switzerland, to buy up approximately U.S. $3 billion within a few days. Finally, these and other smaller countries decided they could not support the dollar any longer. International foreign money exchanges were shut down for days. These countries reasoned that a wholesale conversion, in Europe, of U.S. dollars into European currencies, which were neither wanted or needed, is counterproductive. **This was the case of an instant inflation on a gigantic scale in the U.S.A. and Europe.**

In addition, the Keynesian economic policies, which advocates creating monetary liquidity by governments to support, encourage and sustain economic growth, were advocated in Western Europe. This added more fuel to the raging fire of inflation.

THE NIXON MONETARY POLICY

On August 15, 1971, President Nixon suspended the convertability of the U.S. dollar into gold. The immediate result was a joint upward floating of most major world currencies, in relation to the U.S. dollar. By December 1971, the Bretton Woods Agreement was modified. The so-called Smithsonian Agreement (the meeting was held at the Smithsonian Institution) was reached among the IMF-nations. The U.S. dollar was devalued by increasing the price of gold from $35 to $38 an ounce. Another "innovation" of the Smithsonian Agreement permitted the IMF-nations to let their currencies fluctuate 2 1/4 % up or down from the official price as compared to Bretton Woods' originally established 1% bracket. The U.S. dollar promptly fell to the floor and stayed there.

On February 1973 (just before the October/Ramadan -1973 war) a second devaluation of the U.S. dollar, this time a much more pronounced one, took place. Shortly thereafter, most major Western nations followed the lead of Canada, Germany, Holland and others by allowing their currencies to float against the U.S. dollar. The introduction of the "floating exchange rates" became an accepted fact. As a result, and claiming that speculation contributes to stability, the so-called International Monetary Exchange Market of the Chicago Mercantile Exchange was introduced. Finally, in November 1973, the major countries agreed to "demonetize" gold. The participating IMF major governments agreed to sell gold on the free market to define a fair market value for gold or indeed for the U.S. dollar. **Thus governments were no longer required to hold gold in reserve for the purpose of settling balance-of-payments deficit.**

The IMF is now an active proponent of fiscal and monetary controls in many of the developing countries and the former Eastern European countries as well as the former Soviet republics. The IMF policies are heavily flavored by the policies of the G-7 club of nations. These are the U.S., England, Japan, France, Canada, Italy and Germany.

CHAPTER SEVEN

THE EUROPEAN MONETARY UNION

EUROPE'S ATTEMPT TO REACH POLITICAL UNITY

This chapter is a brief review of Europe's efforts to unite politically. It serves as an introduction to a case study of a group of nations on one continent which tries to integrate their economies, markets and ultimately political systems into what may be called the "United States of Europe." It is felt that these efforts and the experience of Europe in reaching these goals are important lessons for those who want to see the developing Muslim countries' economies, markets and political leadership united. We hope that this entity will be the major force behind offering and proving the usefulness of the LARIBA system as an alternative to the RIBA system in the world.

The European Economic Community- EEC

After WWII, Europe was divided politically and economically into Western Europe, dominated by the U.S., France and

England, and Eastern Europe, dominated by the (former) Soviet Union. Germany was split into West and East and France went along but with subtle resentments to the new and old English-speaking masters of Western Europe (the U.S. and the U.K.).

As the European economies developed in the 50's and 60's, many European leaders, mainly in France under the leadership of Mr. de Gaulle, called for a united Europe. A 12-nation European Economic Community (EEC) was started with its own parliament and economic integration boards of governors including industrial and agricultural policy planning bodies.

The 12-nation EEC focused first on reducing and/or removing trade tariffs, promoting trade amongst Western European countries, and attempting to achieve uniform wage policies in the EEC countries. The U.K. policy makers did not like the idea. They wanted to control Europe through the financial powerhouse of London and to control international trade through monetary planning and exchange rate fluctuations, all originating from the source of world trading in currencies and many commodities; i.e. London.

The Fall of The Soviet Union And The Unification of Germany

With the collapse of the Soviet Union, and the unification of Germany into one potential major power in Europe, the dream of uniting Europe started to gain strength. German political leaders' vision was to see Germany regaining its lost bid for Europe, albeit this time peacefully. Their vision was to see Europe disengaged from the U.S./U.K. political and monetary domination. France liked the idea, and French political leaders under the leadership of President Francois Mitterand promoted a new system called the European Monetary Union (EMU).

The European Monetary Union- An Historic Perspective

The idea is to sweep away trade barriers amongst the E.E.C. countries, and to stimulate economic activity. This union idea is not new, in fact it was tried back in the year 794; the occasion, the Council of Frankfort; and the man who conceived of this union was Charlemagne, the man who was responsible for the stopping of the tide of Islam deep into Europe after taking control of Spain and parts of Southern Europe. The military campaigns that followed his succession in 768 had given him control of an empire stretching from modern-day Austria to the Atlantic. Only Napoleon and Hitler were to emulate his reach. Charlemagne was fascinated by economic policy and the value of his coinage of a standard currency called the denarius(after the Muslim dinar).

Article 5 of the proceedings of the Council of Frankfort reads:

"As regards denarii ... you should be fully aware of a decree that everywhere, in every city and every trading place, the new denarii are also to be legal tender and to be accepted by everybody. And if they bear the monogram of our name and are of pure silver and full weight, should anyone reject, in any place, in any transaction of purchase or sale, he is to pay 15 soldi [roughly the price of a cart load of wheat]".

The new coins were introduced after Charlemagne's crushing defeat of the Avars of Eastern Europe in 791. For the first time since Roman days, Europe's coins were minted with uniform design though Charlemagne's bust was not to be a regular feature until 812. In contrast to earlier practice, fewer than 40 mints across the empire were allowed to produce the new coins; in 812 they were reduced to about ten.

The new money was widely adopted, as if some European monetary system existed. King Offa of Mercia (a small kingdom to Charlemagne's north west) enlarged the size and weight of his pennies broadly in line with Carolinian reforms. Before long, others, including Pope Leo, followed suit.

It was not just the coinage that changed. Before Charlemagne, the economy had centered on feudal gift-giving and subsistence farming. Market place values had largely disappeared with the Romans. Charlemagne's reforms, announced at the Frankfort Council, aimed to tip the balance back towards the market.

Some claim it was made possible by the influx of treasures from the defeated Avars; others that the reform coincided with the discovery of new silver mines in western France. A more elaborate thesis is that Charlemagne obtained the silver as a tribute from the Beneventan and Danish Kings, who were engaged in lucrative commerce with the Abbasid Muslim traders connected to the silver-rich court of Khalifh Harun al-Rashid in Baghdad.

More intriguing, however, than the source of his wealth are Charlemagne's motives. Modern French, German and Italian politicians hark back frequently to the Carolinian achievement. All have been nurtured on the thesis of a Belgian historian, Henri Pirenne, who contends that Charlemagne erected the scaffolding of a medieval Europe which was quite different from the totalitarian regimes of antiquity and which has fascinated generations of historians, philosophers and social scientists.

After Charlemagne's standardization of the coinage, land, already measured in monetary terms, took on new values. The court, the main monasteries and the aristocracy set out to increase the size of their properties, systematically clearing land and concluding written, long-term agreements with tenants to develop agricultural production. Roman technologies were revived. The old tribal ethics of Western Europe was slowly eclipsed by society in which service was the paramount relationship: service on the land; service to knights, king, or emperor; above all services to God.

With monetary reform went a Church-led cultural renaissance, producing books about paintings and new styles of wall paintings, metal works and sculpture. The reform of the coinage, business, and the land went hand-in-hand with this cultural renaissance. By contrast, modern Europe's discussion of monetary reform, with its emphasis on the harmonization of rules rather than the promotion of cultural and social diversity, seems questionable.

Ironically, Charlemagne's court at Aachen was less than 35 miles from the new locations for the latest European Monetary Union, Maastricht.

The central question is, can the developing countries of the world learn from history to bring about a Union of States, clustered in a way that homogenous enough to make a difference in the life of their citizens?

The European Monetary Union (EMU) and The European Exchange Rate Mechanism (ERM)

The Europeans, in an effort to establish a new European block which can stand up to the Japanese and U.S. economic powers, started promoting the idea of working to achieve a unified single currency for Europe. The idea of the "United Europe" movement gained support and momentum when Mr. Bush, the former President of the United States, advanced his "new world divided order" foreign policy. This new order saw the world divided into larger blocks (or clusters) led by a major country in each region. For example, Germany would lead Europe, Japan would lead Asia and South East Asia, Saudi Arabia would lead the Muslim countries, and so on. All of these leader-countries would then be led by the U.S.A.; the only super power of the world. This whole vision was rejected by the policy makers of the U.K. They saw this as a direct threat to the very existence and continuation of the U.K. as the leader of Europe.

The "European Monetary Union" was created because the European policy makers believed that the first step towards real political unity was to stabilize exchange rates through stabilization of monetary policy, then reaching a unified currency for Europe. It was towards this effort that the European Rate Mechanism (ERM) was agreed upon in Maastricht, Holland to become the treaty that governs the exchange rates amongst European currencies.

The European Exchange Rate Mechanism- ERM

The ERM was originally designed as a multilateral system of currencies. In theory, if one country's currency hit its floor against another, then both governments were meant to take remedial action. In practice, the weak currency countries have always been forced to raise their interest rates to keep their exchange rates within its permitted band (2.25% in most cases and can be up to 10% in some cases and 15% in other cases) against the Deutsche Mark; i.e. the anchor currency stipulated by the treaty. This made the Deutsche Mark, officially, the anchor currency of Europe (and not the British pound which was the unofficial anchor currency for a long time). The Deutsche Mark is the worlds second most widely held currency after the U.S. dollar. In 1992, some 75% of European transactions were done in Deutsche Mark. Germany's economy is by far the biggest European economy. It is 50% bigger than France and accounts for more than 40% of the total output of all ERM members.

The U.K. policy makers did not like the agreement. It meant that the U.K. would lose London as the center of all world financial transactions, an honor which would shift to Frankfurt. They balked, but were forced politically to join. In an effort to try to reestablish itself, the Bank of England through political and currency speculation and maneuvering got the British pound to approximately $2 per pound level. The objective was to justify for the British government and the rest of Europe to reduce their interest rates to get the economy in England going and to force the Bundesbank (Germany's Central Bank) to reduce its interest rates hoping to fuel inflation in Germany. The Bundesbank refused and the British, unilaterally, reduced interest rates. The British pound sank from $2 to approximately $1.5 per pound in no time. The Bank of England was required to increase its interest rate to keep with the Maastricht agreement. But they decided to drop out completely. Earlier, attacks by currency speculators drove the Italian Lira out from the system in 1992.

Attacks in the summer of 1993 on other currencies of the ERM (mainly the French Franc) by currency speculators were so overwhelming that the system was, for all practical purposes, dismantled. European currencies can now float by as much as 15%. London's nightmare, called ERM and EMU, is now out for sometime to come. The ERM finally was ratified in October 1993, and Frankfurt was made the headquarters of the European Monetary Institute, Europe's Central Bank.

SECTION III

THE PRACTICAL ASPECTS OF STARTING UP AND OPERATING A LARIBA BANK

In this last section, the book reviews the practical aspects of starting up and operating a LARIBA bank. Chapter 8 reviews the major features of the LARIBA banking policies and practices. The relationship of the LARIBA bank with its depositors and entrepreneurs and business persons, who would utilize the LARIBA bank funds to invest it in the economy, is discussed in Chapter 9. Chapter 10 discusses, in detail, the process of attracting the deposits to the LARIBA bank and the legal (Sharia) relationship between the bank and the depositors. It also discusses the types of deposit services available in the LARIBA banks. The other important and most crucial role of the LARIBA banks' function; i.e. its investing of the funds it accumulates, is discussed in Chapter 11. This chapter explains the different financing models offered by the LARIBA bank and the portfolio management approach that should be used by the LARIBA bank to reduce risk and realize better returns.

Finally Chapter 12 outlines the foundations of the author's dream of a LARIBA banking system which prevails world-wide as an alternative banking system to the RIBA system for the benefit of mankind.

CHAPTER EIGHT

MAJOR FEATURES OF THE ISLAMIC

LARIBA BANKING POLICIES

1. Focuses on the human contribution as a source of income (profits) and limits income from just capital. The LARIBA Bank emphasizes that it is an institution entrusted with the management of capital for the purpose of economic growth through the creation of new job opportunities. It derives its income for such a service as a Mudarib, (money manager for economic growth). The LARIBA Bank stresses the definition of a "commission" or a "management credit" as a remuneration for the work it does. The LARIBA Bank objective is to expand its profits through serving the economic growth targets of the community.

2. Tries to maintain, as much as possible, the role of the LARIBA Bank as an intermediary, i.e. an honest match maker

(broker) between the owners of capital (depositors/investors) and the entrepreneur (business person). The bank's legal status, from an Islamic point of view, is defined on that basis as a Mudarib.

3. Stands ready to be responsible for the outcome of this new approach to banking, i.e. The LARIBA Banking way. This will present to the community at large a living aspect of the application of the Islamic LARIBA system. For that cause the bank shareholders and its employees (workers and managing partners) should be willing to accept to forgo some of the short term higher profits and risk to ensure the success of this new pilot experiment. The financiers in charge of the LARIBA Bank should approach their responsibility not only as business people but also as dedicated and believing leaders for the purpose of realizing a dream. The dream is to apply and bring to life a working Islamic LARIBA financial system, at least on a community level, as one of the pillars of a new world order which operates according to the Islamic principles. This task should be looked upon as a form of Jihad (striving) which requires sacrifices and continuous giving.

The real profits of the LARIBA Bank will not only be measured in dollars and cents. But, in addition, the real profits will be the contributions of the bank to open job opportunities and new businesses. The net result would be more economic activity, growth and affluence of the community.

4. Develops ways and means by which the LARIBA Bank can perform its unique activities without interest. Here, the task requires the dedicated contributions of professionals who

are well versed in Islamic knowledge and who are dedicated Islamically, and who are, at the same time, experts in banking operations and businesses. These professional Muslims would act as the fulfillers of the missing link between Islamic Sharia (jurisprudence) and the banking business. Creative financial products and services development along the lines and rules of LARIBA are going to be the key to the success of the LARIBA Banking system in a world governed by RIBA banking system.

Three issues emerge as we attempt to achieve the goal of developing and building a LARIBA bank. These are:

> 1. How to structure the LARIBA bank in such a way that will allow it not to charge interest on money it pays out to those who need the money (called lending in RIBA banking and investing in LARIBA banks)? As it is well known, the interest on loans represents a major source of income for RIBA banks.

> 2. What should be the relationship between the LARIBA bank and its depositors and entrepreneurs who would be in charge of using the depositors' money to invest it on their behalf (called borrowers in RIBA banking)?

> 3. How will the LARIBA bank compete with the banking services offered by RIBA banks? and what are the alternative services which meet the demands of the community while at the same time comply with the laws of the Islamic LARIBA system?

CHAPTER NINE

RELATIONSHIP OF THE LARIBA BANK WITH ITS DEPOSITORS AND THE USERS OF ITS FUNDS FOR INVESTING

The LARIBA bank obtains its funds from two main sources as compared to the RIBA bank. These are:

1. Shareholders' Capital; which is looked upon as long-term risk money by the shareholders. In addition, the accumulated earnings of the bank, can be reinvested in the bank capital.

2. Depositors' funds from those community individuals and institutions who have a much lower risk tolerance for their capital.

RIBA banks derive their funds from the same sources outlined above. However, a very large source of funds for RIBA banks is the Central Bank of the country where the bank operates. For example, in the U.S. if the shareholders' capital is $100 million, then this RIBA bank can create a lending ability to lend up to 20 times that much; i.e. $2 billion (provided that it abides by other rules and regulations set by the Central Bank; i.e. the Fed in the U.S.). **This represents the most important challenge for the growth and stability of LARIBA banks in a world which operates by Riba concepts.** It is believed that God in the long run will bless those who commit and have small means (as reported by the Prophet's Hadith (saying)). However, prudent planning and management are required to meet the challenge.

In the RIBA banking system the RIBA bank focuses on borrowing money at low interest rates (money market deposits, and/or CD's) or no interest rate (checking account/demand deposits) and then lending the money at a higher interest rate. The spread between the interest earned by the bank on its loans and the interest paid to depositors on their different types of deposits represents a large portion of the profit of the RIBA bank.

The RIBA bank derives its importance from its capacity to accumulate capital from those who own money but are not capable of placing it in productive investments either because they do not have the experience and ability and/or because they are not interested in or can afford assuming the risk of losing their capital. The owners of capital are attracted to the RIBA bank by the level of interest paid to them on their deposits and the insurance supplied, in the U.S.A. for example, by the Federal Deposit Insurance Corporation (FDIC) on their deposits that are less than $100,000.

In this context the RIBA bank's legal relationships can be broken into the following two entities:

1. A legal relationship between the depositors as creditors of the bank and the bank as liable to the depositors.

2. A legal relationship of the bank with the business person/entrepreneur who borrows the money to invest it by putting it to work. In this case, the bank is the creditor and the business persons are liable to the bank.

This way, the bank is not legally looked upon as an intermediary between the owners of capital and the business person who borrows the money for a business activity. In fact, the bank in this context has become a real principal in two different relationships while there exists no relationship between the owner of capital (depositors) and the real user of capital (the borrower).

In LARIBA banking, the bank is looked upon in a different context, this can be conceptualized as follows:

1. If the deposits are looked upon as deposits for Amana (trust), then the bank has no right to dispense the Amana without the prior consent of the depositor. Here comes the question of the effect of inflation and the impact of it on the deposits which after a certain time may have less purchasing power. In fact, if the depositor wants to keep his/her funds without employing them, as an Amana, their deposits not only

decline due to inflation but also because they are required to pay the 2.5% Zakah on them if they are kept unutilized for an economic investment activity of a period of a year or more; Hawl (period/cycle).

2. If the depositors deposit their funds with the purpose of allowing the bank to manage their money on their behalf, then the bank enters into a relationship with depositors as Mudarib (money manager) for the depositors. The most important ingredient in the agreement is the level of risk the depositor is willing to accept. In this context, the depositor becomes an investor. Other ingredients of the Mudaraba agreement (money management agreement) would be the time duration of the investment and the distribution of profits between the bank, Mudarib (money manger) and the owner of capital.

3. If the owner of the capital entrusts the LARIBA bank with searching for business opportunities to invest their capital directly (Direct Investments), then the LARIBA bank takes on the role of an investment banker intermediary who would work on behalf of the owner of the capital and business person for a service fee. Now the relationship is direct between the owner of the capital and the business person. The LARIBA bank's responsibility is mainly the performance of the due diligence to assess the business parameters of the relationship and maybe to structure the deal financially and legally and to make sure that it follows the tenets of Islamic financing of LARIBA.

CHAPTER TEN

DEPOSITS IN LARIBA BANKS

The process of depositing the money with the LARIBA bank; i.e. entrusting the bank with it not as an *Amana* (trust or in safe deposit boxes) but as an investment with the LARIBA bank appointed as a *Mudarib* (money manager) is called *Mudaraba* deposits.

The *Mudaraba* contract is an agreement between the owner of the capital and the money manager *Mudarib* (in this case the LARIBA bank). The use of capital is done through the work of the *Mudarib* or its designated business person. The two entities agree on a distribution formula of the profits of the venture in case the venture is profitable. If there is no profit and no loss, then the owner of capital would recover his/her capital in full. If there is a loss, then the owner of capital incurs all the losses without liability to the *Mudarib*. The *Mudarib* loses the value of time and effort put towards investing the capital. To encourage businessmen to assume the risk, the *Mudaraba* agreement may define a minimum wage for the *Mudarib* to encourage him/her to undertake the responsibility. Of course, the underlying assumption is that the *Mudarib* performs his duties with due diligence and according to the defined articles of the contract.

In summary, the participants of the *Mudaraba* deposit transaction are:

1. The Depositor: owner of capital.

2. The Business person: owner of the idea or business experience; *Aamil* (worker or employed).

3. The LARIBA bank as an intermediary (money manager) between both sides above and as a representative of the depositor for dispensing the funds.

DEPOSITING THE FUND
IN THE LARIBA BANK

Each deposit is (theoretically) characterized as a personal deposit owned by the depositor. The title of the deposit is not transferred to the bank. That means that the LARIBA bank cannot lend it without the permission of the owner as in the case of RIBA banks.

On the other hand, in reality, the deposits are not kept segregated from one another except by the variation of the projected duration of the investment and the level of risk accepted by the owner of the deposit. The LARIBA bank would pool these deposits in a number of pools by the permission and consent of the depositors. Each depositor would own a certain fraction of the pool which is proportional to the deposit.

The LARIBA bank would then act as an investment banker representative (*wakeel*) to dispense the funds from the pool for investment purposes.

In order to motivate the depositors to deposit their money with the RIBA bank, these banks offer the following motivating factors:

1. Customer deposits are guaranteed by the bank (as long as the bank is viable), and in the U.S.A. deposits are insured by a federal government insurance agency, the Federal Deposit Insurance Corporation, FDIC up to $100,000.

2. The income earned by the depositor on his/her deposit is paid in the form of fixed and determined interest rate.

3. The depositor is able to withdraw his/her money at the end of the period or at any time.

The challenge faced by the pioneers of LARIBA banking in a RIBA banking world is to try to come up with creative ways and means to be able to compete with the RIBA banks without violating the *Sharia* (Islamic Jurisprudence).

1. Insuring the Deposits of the LARIBA Bank

The LARIBA bank is allowed by *Sharia* point of view to guarantee the principal and promise to return the deposits of its depositors in its totality. In case the project financed is not profitable, the Sharia stipulates that the worker *Aamil* (businessman) who is in charge of investing the funds cannot guarantee the principal. So, as long as the bank was not participating in the active investing of the funds, the bank can then guarantee the principal. So, if the bank acts as an intermediary between the depositors (pool owner) and the workers (businessmen) *Aamil,* the bank is actually a third party which can volunteer its guarantee to the depositors on their deposits.

2. Income on Deposits (Interest in RIBA banks and Return on Investment in LARIBA banks).

The LARIBA bank would pay a certain percentage of its profits to the depositors (owners of the funds in the pool of capital). Here comes the possibility of project failure or losses. This possibility is minimized to a very low level through diversification by sector (both demography and business activity) and through dispersion to avoid concentration of investment risk with a particular entity.

It should be noted here that the return on deposits should not be less than the interest paid by the RIBA banks. Otherwise, the depositors will fly away from the LARIBA banks to the RIBA bank. In fact, based on the prior operating experience of the LARIBA bank and the opportunity expected rate of return as guided by the competition (RIBA banks), the LARIBA bank should give its customers and depositors an idea about the expected return on their deposits without guarantees.

There are other risks in addition to the major risk discussed above regarding the failure of the project. These are: 1) the risk of slower than expected economic activity, and 2) the risk of not investing the deposits immediately after they have been deposited. That is why it may be recommended to indicate to the depositors that a time lag may occur between the time their deposits are made and the time these deposits get invested. This period can be as long as two months. However, the LARIBA bank should commit to doing all that it can to redeploy the deposits in the economy as soon as deposited.

3. Ability of the Time Depositors to Cash Their Deposits on Demand

The difficulty here is in the ability of the LARIBA bank to keep enough liquidity to pay the premature demand of the term depositors while most of the deposits are invested in medium and long-term projects. This issue is the most important issue regarding the credibility of any bank. In fact, if any bank fails to meet the demands of its depositors, the damage done will be serious, irreversible and may mean the closure of such bank. In the RIBA banking system, they developed a lender of last resort; i.e. the Central Bank. But because the LARIBA system does not have a lender of last resort, it is important for the LARIBA bank, at least for now, to employ a chief financial officer who would develop a model that is capable of projecting the cash flow of the LARIBA bank and in the same time project the different maturities of the different investments authorized by the bank. The following should be taken in consideration:

3.1. During the start-up of the bank (the first 10 years), the LARIBA bank should finance projects with maturities ranging between 3 months and 3 years in the first 2 years of operation, 3 months and 5 years in the following 3 years and then 3 months and 7 years in the following 5 years. This way, cash will always be available for unexpected withdrawals and/or reinvestment.

3.2. The shareholders of the LARIBA bank should stand ready to meet any run on the bank deposits. This in itself will make the shareholders, who are in the same time the managing directors of the LARIBA bank, careful about reviewing the assets/liabilities management and cash flow projections by the chief financial officer.

3.3. The commercial entities and individuals who seek financing from the LARIBA bank should be required to keep a balance on deposit as an investment with the LARIBA bank, with the bank having the right to offset it against the financing facility (loan in RIBA banks). This investment deposit can be built up over time.

3.4. The LARIBA bank executive committee should keep liquidity reserves to meet expected demands on deposits as well as additional reserves for unexpected demands. The level of such reserves can be obtained from operating experience of the LARIBA bank. But the most important factor here is the close and continual contact with every depositor, investor, entrepreneurs and other clients of the bank. If these contacts are developed to reach the level of a big family, then projections about the demands of the members of the family can be assessed in advance without any unpleasant surprises.

3.5 As the LARIBA banking system develops into numerous branches and outlets, they can develop amongst themselves, a central banking authority and a deposit protection authority to become the "lender of last resort" (actually supplier of liquidity in case a run on a member LARIBA bank is experienced).

TYPES OF DEPOSITS IN THE LARIBA BANK

In order to organize the deposits/investments (Assets/Liability) management of the LARIBA bank, it may prove useful, based on our experience, to offer the investors the following three categories of deposits to meet the competition offered by RIBA banks:

1. Demand Deposits-*Amana*

These are deposits kept with the LARIBA bank for safekeeping. The money can be withdrawn on demand. Because these deposits are looked upon from a jurisprudence, *Sharia,* point of view as an *Amana (trust),* then the money cannot be invested. A fee can be charged by the LARIBA bank for the service. The level of the fee is left for the LARIBA bank management to decide based upon specific condition. The withdrawal can be conducted by proper authorization through check writing and/or telephone (wire) authorization providing that proper written agreements are signed. In LARIBA banking, all relationships should be formalized in the form of a written contract, *Aqd,* as prescribed and required by the Holy Qur'an.

2. Time Deposits

To compete with the certificate of deposits (CD's) service offered by RIBA banks, the LARIBA bank can offer the prospective depositors various portfolios, *Mahfaza* of investments with an expected maturity and expected rate of return. This way the LARIBA bank financial manager can better plan and organize his/her total portfolio. Premature demands for withdrawals can be met. However, all administrative and legal costs involved in the adjustments of the portfolio as well as the cost of raising of the matching liquidity to meet the demand should be charged. In case of RIBA banks, a penalty is charged. In case of LARIBA banks actual costs should be applied. A detailed outline of the costs should be made clear to the depositors at the time of making such deposits.

3. Investments

To compete with the Money Market Account type of deposits offered by the RIBA bank, the LARIBA bank can offer open ended deposits. However, it is important to ask the investor to indicate in writing their expectations for the need of such deposits; i.e. time horizon of such an investment. In addition, the investment agreement should stipulate that the investor should give the LARIBA bank enough time to meet their demand on their deposits. This can be two weeks to two months depending on the assets of the LARIBA bank, the maturity and operating experience of its operations and most importantly the size of the investment.

4. Savings

These accounts can be looked upon in the same way as investment type deposits. However, in this case the objective of the savings account holder should be clearly delineated. For example, if it is opened to save for retirement, savings for future monthly income, saving for purchase of a home, saving for children education, saving for pilgrimage *Haj,* or saving for spending in the cause of God. The definition of the objectives of the savings will give the chief financial officer of the LARIBA bank an estimate of the cash flow projections of the bank assets and liabilities. This will minimize the potential negative impact of a severe run on the LARIBA bank and will make it easier on the budgeting process regarding the kinds and investment duration of the investments financed by the LARIBA bank.

As the picture of the different types of deposits become better defined, the chief financial officer of the LARIBA bank would be better equipped to budget and manage the funds of the bank for the other side of the bank activities and that is: investing of the bank deposits.

CHAPTER ELEVEN

INVESTING THE LARIBA BANK DEPOSITS

As the LARIBA bank accumulates deposits, the most important next step is to employ that capital in a productive way to generate economic activity which in turn will generate profit, employment opportunities and more affluence for the community. The investments department of the LARIBA bank can be looked upon as a finder of good investments for the purpose of enhancing the economic well being of the community leading to its financial independence. The LARIBA bank investment officers (called loan officers in RIBA banks) can be looked upon as investment bankers and as development bankers. In his/her capacity as an investment banker, he/she is responsible for finding investment opportunities for the owner of capital. In this case he/she would match the risk level acceptable to the owners of capital and their investment objectives with investment opportunities available in the community. This activity is rewarded in the form of a finders' credit. The owner of capital would enter into a direct investment agreement with the owner of the investment idea and/or business person,

Aamil, with the LARIBA bank acting as an intermediary (broker) and if agreeable as manager of that relationship. In his/her capacity as a manager of the relationship the LARIBA bank would follow-up on the progress of the investment and the adherence of the *Aamil* to the conditions of the investment agreement, and can collect the profits due to the owner of the capital. These and other services would be conducted by the LARIBA bank for a service fee agreed upon by the three parties; i.e. the owner of capital, the *Aamil* and the LARIBA bank.

The LARIBA bank can also act as a trustee on the deposited funds as well as a *Mudarib* of some of the deposits (only for depositors who allow *Mudaraba* using their deposits) and of the shareholders capital. In this capacity the LARIBA bank would realize a service fee as well as participation in the profits/loss of the investments.

LARIBA FINANCING MODELS

1. Murabaha (Cost Plus)

In a *Murabaha* contract the client would approach the LARIBA bank to finance the purchase of a certain item. Because the client does not have the funds, the bank would buy that item in response to the order of the client. The title of that item transfers from the seller to the LARIBA bank. Then, the LARIBA bank would have another sales agreement to sell the item to the client at a price which includes a profit element. As a result of this sales step, the title transfers from the LARIBA bank to the client. The total sales price (including the LARIBA bank's profit) would be paid back to the LARIBA bank over a period of time. It is important to note that the sale price agreed upon between the LARIBA bank and the client is final. Following are some questions about special situations which may arise in such dealings:

1.1 How Does the LARIBA Bank Define its Profit?

The LARIBA bank, in its efforts to return an acceptable profit for its shareholders and investors, would study the market and the competition. One important competition would be the RIBA banks and the products they offer for investors of capital. For example, the interest rates paid by RIBA banks on certificates of deposit, savings accounts and money market instruments. And because the LARIBA bank's objective is to return to its investors and shareholders a superior return (by 1.5-2%) over the interest paid by RIBA banks, this will define the opportunity rate of return expected by the owners of capital. On the other hand, the LARIBA bank, in its effort to enhance its credibility with its customers, should advise its customers to shop around for the best available financing in the market. This way, the LARIBA bank investment/finance committee would develop a range for the profit to be negotiated with the customer. The LARIBA bank should make it clear in its negotiations that this profit is not of the same nature as that charged, in the form of interest, by the RIBA banks. It should also be noted that the LARIBA bank officer should show the customer in dollars and cents the difference between the customer's cost of financing using LARIBA and RIBA.

Then comes the question to the customer: "what is your choice? You (the customer) have a choice between RIBA and LARIBA–the final decision is yours."

1.2. What If the Customer Wants to Accelerate His/Her Payments?

In RIBA banking, a time-value of money is applied. Hence, if the customer wants to prepay, the time value is applied. The customer pays less and maybe a prepayment fee. In this case, the client can save some money. This concept is not accepted from a *Sharia* (jurisprudence) point of view in LARIBA banking. However, in case that happens, the LARIBA bank may include in the sales agreement a renegotiation clause to renegotiate the price in case of accelerated payments. In addition, the time spent by the finance, the accounting and legal officers, in addition to any out-of-pocket expenses by the LARIBA bank should be charged.

1.3. What If the Customer Cannot Make the Payment and Honor the Contract?

This is the very unhappy situation in any financial institution RIBA or LARIBA. The reason for the customer's inability to honor his/her contract may be one of the following:

> 1.3.1. The customer over-extended him/herself by expanding his/her activities and/or consumptive behavior beyond his/her means. If this is the case, then it is the error of the

LARIBA bank which was supposed to do an in-depth analysis of the customer's cash flow. Of course, these situations can be specific and they vary from one customer to another. However, the LARIBA bank should work with the customer and make a conscious decision as to how to help the customer meet his/her obligations. Maybe this can be achieved through prolonging the repayment without charging any additional cost of money as is done by RIBA banks. The only additional charges allowed are out of pocket expenses by the LARIBA bank, and the officers' time incurred in restructuring the contract. If a person who has financed a car, for instance, repeatedly fails to make his/her payments then the car is re-possessed. The car is sold in the market and if there is a credit due to the client, the money is paid back. If there is a deficit, then the loss is LARIBA bank's loss.

1.3.2. The customer is faced with an unexpected calamity like, for example, losing his/her job. In this case the customer is treated the same way as in 1.3.1 above. The LARIBA bank, out of its good will, may decide to forgo any additional expenses and costs by donating the LARIBA bank expenses and officer's time as part of its Zakah (*Gharimoon*- heavily indebted- category).

1.4 What If the Client was Found to Have Misrepresented Facts or to Have Given Incorrect Information?

This is the time when the LARIBA bank has the right to withdraw the item financed. The client is pursued to the fullest by the LARIBA bank in order to recover as much of the loss as possible. Additionally, all out of pocket expenses should be charged to the client.

2. Leasing (Ajara)

Here, the LARIBA Bank would own title to the item financed. At the request of the client, the bank would purchase the item and lease it back to the client for a predefined term.

Here one needs to differentiate between financial leases and capital leases as defined in RIBA financing. In LARIBA financing, the lease would be defined by a certain period, usually 3, 5 or 7 years depending on the nature of the project or item leased. At the end of the lease, the contract may stipulate that the client may have the option to buy the item at fair market value or the item would revert to the LARIBA bank to sell it in the market.

In practical terms, the lease profitability is defined by asking the client to shop around for competitive leases in the market. In most leases the LARIBA bank, because of its lower overhead and lower loans losses, would be able to compete and lease the item at a lower rate than what the competition charges.

3. Lease/Purchase - Ajara/Imtilak

In this model the LARIBA bank would enter into a joint agreement with the client to buy an item. For example the LARIBA bank would own 75% of the item and the client 25% of the item. The lease rate is defined as the market dictates. The 25% portion of the lease payment due to the client can be paid to the LARIBA bank to reduce the bank's equity and increase the client's equity, such that after a certain time the client owns the whole item.

4. Joint Venture - Musharaka (Direct Investment/Equity ownership)

In this model the LARIBA bank or its investment subsidiary enters into direct investment in equity form with the other parties or clients. Profit and/or loss would be assigned to each joint venture according to a well defined distribution formula.

5. Money Management - Mudaraba

Here the LARIBA bank itself can act as a money manager through its investment banking finance/investment advisory board. The bank can also delegate that function (as a *Wakeel*) to other money managers.

The Mudaraba contract would stipulate the responsibility of the bank as a Mudarib (money manager) or as a *Wakeel* (representative with discretionary authority) of the client to find a money manager who will meet the risk level defined by the client and his/her other investment objectives.

Ultimately, the LARIBA bank, as it matures, would be involved in *Mudaraba* business in most of its businesses.

In the *Mudaraba* agreement the LARIBA bank can act in one of two capacities. The first as a representative on behalf of the client (depositors). In this case it would charge a small fee as a remuneration for its servicing the account. The other would be as an active *Mudarib* (money manager). Here the LARIBA bank can invest its own capital along with the capital of the clients. Here the bank can participate in the profit/loss through its capital participation. However, it can also participate in the profit realized from the client portion of the investment according to a predetermined formula. In case of loss, the LARIBA bank would incur losses on its capital participation but would not assume any of the losses due to the client, assuming that the LARIBA bank has done its due diligence and evaluation of the venture. The LARIBA bank, however, can charge a service fee to the client to pay for the cost of servicing the account.

6.Advanced Purchasing of Future Production - Futures - *Baii Salam*

In this model the LARIBA bank would come to an agreement to buy the production of an orchard, a farm or an item like equipment or automobiles, ahead of its production at an agreed-upon price. The money is paid in advance to the producer. The producer, in turn, would use the money as a working capital to purchase the basic services, pay wages and buy raw materials necessary for the production. In this model the bank would help in the growth of the economy by providing the liquidity necessary for economic growth.

THE STEP-WISE APPROACH TO RISK MANAGEMENT FOR A LARIBA BANK START-UP

It is important here to stress the importance of risk management for the LARIBA bank. It should be stressed that the credibility and performance of the LARIBA bank are not only professional duties but also an Islamic requirement. The simple fact is that a LARIBA bank should not be allowed to fail or lose people's money. If that happens, then the dream will die for the next 3 to 4 generations. We simply cannot and should not allow this to happen.

Areas of risk management are:

1. LARIBA model used in the financing.
2. Diversification by client.
3. Diversification by sector.
4. Diversification by geographic location.

1. Risk Management By Applying The Proper LARIBA Financing Model

As indicated above, *Murabaha* (cost plus) represents the least risky of the LARIBA financing model. It is true that the profitability may be limited, and that the *Murabaha* model itself is not accepted by some quarters in the LARIBA financing field, but it offers a lowest risk type of investment. The risk grows as we move from *Murabaha* to Baii *Salam.*

It is recommended that the LARIBA bank, in its infancy (first 5-7 years of operation) uses *Murabaha* and *Ajara* leasing as its primary models of financing with the intention of slowly moving forward to joint venturing (*Musharaka*), and *Baii Salam* (futures contract). During these first 5-7 years, the LARIBA bank management should set aside sufficient reserves to allow it to progress towards the other forms of LARIBA financing models. This way, the risk is minimized.

2. Risk Management Through Diversification by Clients

Here, the LARIBA bank management should do its best to spread its financing activity throughout the community without concentrating the financing into a small number of already successful business persons. This way the LARIBA bank activity would be dispersed throughout the community which may result in more clients on the investment side. On the other hand, the probability of failure is distributed over a larger number of clients.

3. Risk Management Through Diversification by Sector

This is what will create the unique character of the LARIBA bank. It is advisable to recruit a viable board of directors for the LARIBA bank which represents the business sectors to be financed by the bank. It is also important that the LARIBA bank, through its analysis of the economic activity as well as political, financial and monetary developments, formulates an investment position on a quarterly basis. In this analysis attractive sectors should be identified as well as non-attractive sectors. This way the Credit Policies Committee of the LARIBA bank would devise an investment "pie" allocating how much of its funds should be invested in each sector. The allocation would be dynamic and would change as the economic environment and projections change.

4. Risk Management Through Diversification By Geographic Location

A close watch should be exercised by the LARIBA bank on the locations which it is interested in. For example, if one is in the U.S., risk factors should be assessed for different states and major cities to allocate how much of the capital should be allocated in each location based on that risk factor. If the bank is investing world-wide then the allocation would be by country and on the basis of the risk-reward of investing in that country.

CHAPTER TWELVE

THE DREAM: A WORLD-WIDE LARIBA BANKING SYSTEM

Our dream is to establish a world-wide LARIBA banking system which will be the driving force behind the economic growth of the community, its political and financial affluence and most importantly the integration of the markets world-wide.

Our dream is to establish a small size ($5-20 million) LARIBA bank or finance company in each community. For example, in the U.S., it should be in every city. Then a state LARIBA bank or finance company would be the integrator of all these small community LARIBA banks. Then a U.S. LARIBA Bank or finance company which will include all the LARIBA banks. The state and country banks would become the "lenders of last resort" which could rescue any of the smaller community LARIBA banks in case it experiences a run on its reserves. Ideally, many country LARIBA banks would integrate into a world LARIBA bank which would eventually be the super LARIBA bank of the World.

Such a structure would provide the syndication power to finance any size project, the networking powers of world-wide synergism of industrial, agricultural, social and educational development world-wide.

It is true that this may be an ambitious dream. However, we need to plan for the next 100 years. The best way of doing this is to start a successful, proven model in our community which will train the youths in LARIBA banking and create a new generation of highly qualified international LARIBA bankers who would be the new "anchor" persons to run the new LARIBA banks in new communities and countries world-wide.

GLOSSARY

OF

ISLAMIC

WORDS

GLOSSARY OF ISLAMIC WORDS

Aamil Worker, Business Manager

Adl Justice

Ajara Leasing model of LARIBA financing

Allah The Name (*al-ism*) of Majesty (*jalalah*), and the "Supreme Name" (*al-ismal-a zam*). Allah is the Name of Essence, or the Absolute. It is possibly contraction of *al-ilah* ('the Divinity"); nevertheless, the word Allah cannot be reduced to theoretical grammatical components. If it is, so to speak, a synthesis of two words, the article al and the word *ilah* ("Divinity") that synthesis, which took place in this world out of the inner logic of Arabic language, was a re-evaluation hidden in the origin of the Arabic language itself. It re-constituted in language a Reality that surpasses incomparably the dimension of the words it apparently contains. The word Allah is a proper and the true Name of God, through which man calls Him personally. It is an opening on to the Divine Essence, beyond language and the world itself.

The Name was known and used before the Qur'an was revealed; for example the name of the Prophet's father was Abd Allah, or the "servant of God." The Name Allah is not confined to Islam alone; it is also the Name by which Arabic-speaking Christians of the Oriental churches call upon God. When written, the

110

Name usually followed by the formula *'azza wa jall* ("Great and Majestic"), or by *jalla jalaluh* ("Great his Majesty").

Alnas The people, the closest word in English is the masses.

Amana Honesty

Amanah Trustworthiness and Trust.

Aqd Contract

Baii-Salam Futures sales contract model of LARIBA financing.

Bukhl Misery, withholding time, resources and advice and not sharing with others.

Duaa Supplication and communication with God to Ask Him almighty.

Falah Salvation

Fard Kifaya An additional zakah ordered by the leader of the Muslim nation to supplement the income of the house of treasury in case of a shortfall.

Gharimoon Those who are legitimately heavily indebted but cannot meet their debt due to unexpected circumstances.

Hadith (lit. "speech","report","account") Specifically, traditions relating to the deeds and utterances of the Prophet as recounted by his Companions. Hadith are divided into two groups: *hadith qudsi* ("sacred Hadith"), in which God Himself is speaking in, as it were, a complementary revelation through the Prophet, and *hadith sharif* ("noble Hadith"), the Prophet's own acts and utterances. Hadith may enunciate doctrine or provide a commentary upon it. They deal with the contents of the Qur'an, social and religious life, and everyday conduct. They are the basis, second only to the Qur'an, for Islamic Law (*shari'ah*).

Halal (lit. "released" [from prohibition]). That which is lawful, particularly income, personal activities, food, and meat from animals that have been ritually slaughtered. The opposite is *haram.*

Haram (lit. "forbidden", for revealed, i.e. sacred, reasons). That which is prohibited. In fiqh (jurisprudence) all actions fall into one of five categories: prohibited (*haram*), discouraged (*makruh*), neutral (*mubah*), recommended (*mustahabb*), and obligatory (*fard*).

Hawl Period, cycle

Hirs Greed

Ibada A technical term in theology meaning acts of worship or ritual, from the verb 'abd "slave", "servitor".

Ihsan (lit. "virtue", "excellence", "making beautiful"). The third element in the canonical definition of Islam as:

112

belief (*iman*) practice (*islam*), and virtue (*ihsan*). Ihsan is explained by the Hadith: "worship God as if you saw Him, because if you do not see Him, nevertheless He sees you.

Ihsan also refers to excellence in what we do. The Prophet said: "Allah has prescribed *ihsan* for everything".

Ihtikaar Hoarding

Iktinaz Hoarding of wealth

Imtilak Ownership of Title

Infaq Spending the dearest of assets if not all for the cause of God. It is the highest level of believing in God.

Iqtisad Moderation

Israf Extravagant spending- those who spend beyond their means and needs, The Qur'an puts them in the company of satan.

Istislah (lit. "Seeking what is correct, wholesome") A principle invoked by the jurist Malik ibn Anas, to the effect that public and individual good must be the criterion for the development of the law. The basis of law is Divine injunction as found in the Qur'an and Sunnah. These canonic sources, however, make implicit only the frame work of Islamic law; the rest being elaborated by such guiding principles as *istislah* or *istihsan.*

Itihad Unity

Khalif (Ar. *khalifah,* "successor", "substitute", "lieutenant",). The Qur'an (2:30) refers to Adam as the embodiments of the *fitrah,* or primordial norm, and as the Khalif , representative or primordial norm, and as the Khalif, representative or vicegerent (*khalifah*), of God on earth. Hence, man in his real nature, and not his fallen one, is cast in the role of viceroy to God. The Prophet , however, was the Khalif of God in the Adamic sense, although his successors could lay claim to the title only insofar as they were his representatives, and carried on his functions as spiritual head and temporal ruler of the Islamic state.

Khilafah The system of Government in Islam headed by the Khalifah.

Lariba Consists of LA meaning No and RIBA, i.e. NO RIBA.

Mahfaza Portfolio

Mudaraba Money Management

Mudarib Money Manager

Murabaha Cost Plus LARIBA financing model

Musharaka Joint Venture

Qur'an (Ar. *al-qur'an,* lit. the "reading", or the "recitation"). The holy book of Islam, the Qur'an is commonly also called the *mus'haf* ("collection of pages", "scripture"), *al-furkan,* (lit the "discrimination" -between truth and unreality), *al-Kitab,* ("the book"), *adh-dhikr* ("the

Rememberence") and many other names. In formal speech it is called *al-qur'an al-karim* ("the Noble Qur'an"), or *al-qur'an al-majid* ("the Glorious Qur'an")

The Qur'an was revealed by God in a form of unique Arabic. Its language became the basis of formal or classical Arabic, both literary and spoken, but while unquestionably the standard, its style is nevertheless inimitable.

Riba (from the root raba: "to grow, increase, exceed"). Usury or profit-interest-from the loan of money or goods, which is prohibited in any degree. Today the prohibition is hardly observed in any Islamic country. Either it is simply disregarded-the Egyptian Mufti Muhammad 'Abduh once declared "moderate interest" lawful - or else it is referred to by some such euphemism as "commission". To stay within the letter of the religious law and soothe consciences, some banks offer the solution of mudarabah (asset management): this defines the placing of capital as a co-investment, which naturally brings a return to both parties.

S -"Sal'la Allahu alayhi Wa Sal'lam" - May the peace and prayers of God be upon him.

Sabr Patience, the best manifestation of believing in God.

Sharia (from the root shara'a "to introduce", "enact", "prescribe".) Reveled law also called *shar'* and *shir'ah.* The canonical law of Islam as put forth in the Qur'an and the Sunnah and elaborated by the analytical principles of the schools of thoughts of Islam

(*madhhab, pl. madhahib*)

Sunnah (lit. "custom", "wont", "usage", pl. *sunan*). A general term that can be applied to the usages and customs of nations, predominant meaning of Sunnah is that of the spoken and acted example of the Prophet Muhammad (S). It includes what he approved, allowed, or condoned when, under prevailing circumstances, he might well have taken issue with others' actions, decisions or practices; and what he himself refrained from and disapproved of.

The Sunnah is the crucial complement to the Qur'an.

Tawhid (the verbal noun of *wahhada,* "to make one" or " to declare or acknowledge oneness"). The acknowledging of the Unity of God, the indivisible, Absolute and the sole Real. This doctrine is central to Islam and, indeed, it is the basis of salvation, but is understood within Islam in two diametrically opposed ways, as it were, that of exclusivity and that of inconclusivity.

Wakeel Representative or Trustee

Zakah (taken to mean "purification" from the verb *zaka* which signifies "to thrive", "to be wholesome", "to be pure"). The giving up of a portion of the wealth one may possess, in excess of what is needed for sustenance, to "purify" or legitimize what one retains. *Zakah* is one of the Five Pillars and is in effect a tax on one's possessions. It may be paid directly to the poor as alms, or to travellers, or to the state. *Zakah* may be used for up keep of the poor, for those who own less than that prescribed for the paying of zakah and who have no earning capacity; for the destitute; Muslims in debt through pressing circumstances; travellers in need; those serving the cause of Islam, and fighting in the way of God (*al-mukatilun fi sabil Allah*); for slaves to buy themselves out of bondage; for benevolent works. Those who collect tax on behalf of the state for disbursement are also allowed to take the needs of their livelihood from it.

The amount due varies according to different kinds of properties. A contribution in kind, whose minimum schedule is called *nisbah,* is specified on numbers of livestock according to species but only on those which are freely pastured and not used for the immediate needs of the household or as a work animals. On land it is the *'ushr,* or tenth, of its produce, although further refinements exist in regard to different grains, irrigated and non-irrigated lands, etc. On gold and silver, that is, liquid assets, to which are also assimilated merchandise, financial instruments, stocks and bonds, beyond an untaxed franchise of "200 dinars", the nisbah is 2.5 % of that value which has been held for one year. On the other hand, alms need not be limited to the legal minimums; what is paid over the legal minimum is *sadaqah;* while benevolent, it is also recommended as a pious and expiatory act.

The person liable for *zakah* must be Muslim and not indebted to the value of the worth upon which the tax is due. Tithe is not due upon personal dwellings. It is possessions, furniture , tools, and instruments, riding and draft animals etc.

The *zakah al-fitr*, more commonly known as *fitrah,* is almost always paid by the pious, roughly equivalent to a quart of grain per person in a household, paid directly to the needy at the end of *Ramadan.* It is equivalent to approximately a good size quality meal, i.e. $10.00 per person.

Zulm Injustice

LIST OF REFERENCES

1   Siddiqui, M.N., Muslim Economic Thinking, Islamic Foundation, Leicester, England 1981

2   Khan, M.A., Islamic Economics: Annotated Sources in English and Urdu, Islamic Foundation, Leicester, England, 1983.

3   Zaman, H.S.M., Journal of Research in Islamic Economics, 1 (2), 51-53 (Winter 1984)

4   Journal of Research in Islamic Economics, 1 (2), 55-61 (Winter 1984)

5   Siddiqui, M.N., Issues in Islamic Banking,, Islamic Foundation, Leicester, 1983, p.23.

6   Toffler, A., The Third Wave, Bantam, New York (1980)

7   Chapra, U., Towards a Just Monetary System, Islamic Foundation, Leicester, England (1985)

8   Naqvi, S.N.H., Ethics and Economics: An Islamic Synthesis, Islamic Foundation, Leicester, England (1981)

APPENDIX
VERSES PERTAINING TO RIBA FROM THE HOLY QURAN

Those who swallow RIBA(usury) cannot rise up save as he ariseth who the devil hath prostrated by (his) touch. That is because they say: Trade is just like RIBA(usury); where-as · Allah permitteth trading and forbiddeth RIBA(usury). He unto who an admonition from his Lord cometh and (he) refraineth (in obedience there-to), he shall keep (the profits of) that which is past, and his affair (henceforth) is with Allah. As for him who returneth (to usury)–Such are rightful owners of the Fire. They will abide therein.

(Chapter II Verse 275)

اَلَّذِيْنَ يَأْكُلُوْنَ الرِّبٰوا لَا يَقُوْمُوْنَ اِلَّا كَمَا يَقُوْمُ الَّذِيْ يَتَخَبَّطُهُ الشَّيْطٰنُ مِنَ الْمَسِّ ذٰلِكَ بِأَنَّهُمْ قَالُوْا اِنَّمَا الْبَيْعُ مِثْلُ الرِّبٰوا وَأَحَلَّ اللهُ الْبَيْعَ وَحَرَّمَ الرِّبٰوا فَمَنْ جَاءَهُ مَوْعِظَةٌ مِّنْ رَّبِّهِ فَانْتَهٰى فَلَهُ مَا سَلَفَ وَأَمْرُهُ اِلَى اللهِ وَمَنْ عَادَ فَأُولٰئِكَ أَصْحٰبُ النَّارِ هُمْ فِيْهَا خٰلِدُوْنَ ۝

Allah hath blighted RIBA(usury) and made almsgiving fruitful. Allah loveth not the impious and guilty.

(Chapter II Verse 276)

يَمْحَقُ اللهُ الرِّبٰوا وَيُرْبِى الصَّدَقٰتِ وَاللهُ لَا يُحِبُّ كُلَّ كَفَّارٍ اَثِيْمٍ ۝

O ye who believe! Observe your duty to Allah, and give up what remaineth (due to you) from RIBA(usury), if ye are (in truth) believers.

(Chapter II Verse 278)

يٰٓاَيُّهَا الَّذِيْنَ اٰمَنُوا اتَّقُوا اللهَ وَذَرُوْا مَا بَقِيَ مِنَ الرِّبٰوٓا اِنْ كُنْتُمْ مُّؤْمِنِيْنَ ۝

And if ye do not, Then be warned of war (against you) from Allah and His messengers. And if ye repent, then ye have your principal (without interest). Wrong not and ye shall not be wronged.

(Chapter II Verse 278)

فَاِنْ لَّمْ تَفْعَلُوْا فَأْذَنُوْا بِحَرْبٍ مِّنَ اللهِ وَرَسُوْلِهِ وَاِنْ تُبْتُمْ فَلَكُمْ رُءُوْسُ اَمْوَالِكُمْ لَا تَظْلِمُوْنَ وَلَا تُظْلَمُوْنَ ۝

121

O ye who believe! Devour not RIBA(usury), doubling and quadrupling (the sum lent).Observe your duty to Allah, that ye may be successful.
(Chapter III Verse 130)

يَاۤأَيُّهَا الَّذِينَ اٰمَنُوا لَا تَاْكُلُوا الرِّبَوٰا اَضْعَافًا مُّضَعَفَةً وَّاتَّقُوا اللّٰهَ لَعَلَّكُمْ تُفْلِحُونَ ۝

And of their taking RIBA(usury) when they were forbidden it, and of their devouring people's wealth by false pretences. We have prepared for those of them who disbelieve a painful doom.
(Chapter IV Verse 161)

وَّاَخْذِهِمُ الرِّبَوٰا وَقَدْ نُهُوۡا عَنْهُ وَ اَكْلِهِمْ اَمْوَالَ النَّاسِ بِالْبَاطِلِ وَ اَعْتَدْنَا لِلْكٰفِرِينَ مِنْهُمْ عَذَابًا اَلِيْمًا۝

That which ye give in RIBA(usury) in order that it may increase on (other) people's property hath no increase with Allah; but that which ye give in charity, seeking Allah's countenance, hath increase manifold.
(Chapter XXX Verse 39)

وَمَاۤ اٰتَيْتُمْ مِّنْ رِّبًا لِّيَرْبُوَا فِيۤ اَمْوَالِ النَّاسِ فَلَا يَرْبُوا عِنْدَ اللّٰهِ وَمَاۤ اٰتَيْتُمْ مِّنْ زَكٰوةٍ تُرِيدُونَ وَجْهَ اللّٰهِ فَاُولٰٓئِكَ هُمُ الْمُضْعِفُونَ ۝

Index